"Soul Empowerment is filled with a wealth of material on soul growth. I have known Rosalie Deer Heart and Michael Bradford for some years and have witnessed their inspiring work with healing. In this new book, they present priceless insights into the spiritual understanding of power and powerlessness, personality strategies versus soul qualities, and much more. Soul Empowerment is truly a 'gift of empowerment' bearing hidden treasures that will benefit novices as well as advanced healers. I highly recommend this book."

—Audrey McGinnis
Unity Minister

Also by Rosalie Deer Heart and Michael Bradford:

Healing Grief: A Mother's Story by Rosalie Deer Heart
The Healing Energy of Your Hands by Michael Bradford

SOUL EMPOWERMENT

A Guidebook for Healing Yourself
and Others

Published in the US by: Heart Link Publications
PO Box 273, San Cristobal, NM 87564

Edited by Ellen Kleiner
Book layout and cover design by David Gregson

Printed in the USA

The ideas, suggestions, and healing techniques in this book are not intended
as a substitute for professional medical treatment. Any application of these
ideas, suggestions, and techniques is at the reader's sole discretion.

Publisher's Cataloging-in-Publication

Heart, Rosalie Deer.
Soul empowerment : a guidebook for healing yourself and others /
Rosalie Deer Heart and Michael Bradford.
p. cm.
Includes bibliographical references and index.
Preassigned LCCN: 97-71512
ISBN: 0-9651576-1-X

1. Self-actualization (Psychology) 2. Healing.
3. Reincarnation therapy. I. Bradford, Michael. II. Title.

BF637.S4H43 1997 158.1
QB197-680

10 9 8 7 6 5 4 3 2 1

SOUL EMPOWERMENT

A GUIDEBOOK FOR HEALING YOURSELF AND OTHERS

Rosalie Deer Heart

&

Michael Bradford

Foreword by Eileen Caddy

Contents

• •

WE DEDICATE THIS BOOK

TO ALL THE

MULTIDIMENSIONAL BEINGS OF LIGHT

WHO HAVE COMMITTED THEMSELVES

TO ASSISTING THE HEALING

OF EARTH MOTHER

AND HER PEOPLE

• •

In Gratitude

Our deepest and lightest gratitude to Ellen Kleiner, our devoted editor and friend, who tracked us down in Mexico, Scotland, and England with recommendations, edited pages, and loving attention. Thank you for committing three months of your life to using your editor's magic on each page of this book.

Loving appreciation to Thierry and Karin Bogliolo of Findhorn Press, who not only patiently mentored us through the copublishing of this book but also volunteered their experience, expertise, and humor to our future endeavors.

Heartfelt joy and awe to the millions of fish that shared the bay with us in Puerto Angel, Oaxaca, Mexico, adding to our relaxation and rejuvenation as we snorkeled between chapters.

FOREWORD

Michael Bradford and Rosalie Deer Heart have given us a very helpful, uplifting and invaluable book in *Soul Empowerment*. This book can be used as a do-it-yourself manual for healing, unconditional love and unconditional thinking. Michael and Rosalie have been very open and honest in their writing, and give excellent examples of how they have used their methods of healing, sharing their many successes as well as some failures.

I found the question and answer section particularly helpful. To be able to use their methods of healing needs deep faith, and belief in one's intuition. I rejoice that they make it very clear that it is God, through them, who does the healing, and that a positive attitude and consciousness of the person being healed is also essential.

I can highly recommend *Soul Empowerment* for anyone who is deeply interested in healing, as I am sure most of us are. We all long for wholeness not only in ourselves but for all humanity.

With love and blessings,

Eileen

Eileen Caddy
Co-founder of the Findhorn Foundation

PREFACE

Writing this book has been an evolutionary stretch for both of us. In late 1993, after working together for quite some time, we decided to write a book about the concepts and techniques that promote soul empowerment. But we were both too identified with our personalities and too unattuned to our essences to collaborate. We completed the outline and ended our relationship.

Over the next two years we lived separate lives in different parts of the world. Although we each kept a copy of the material we had written, neither of us took the initiative to flesh it out for publication. We both continued to teach, however, and to clarify many of the principles of soul empowerment—Rosalie, in the United States and Canada, and Michael, in Europe.

In January 1996 we met again and vowed to complete the book together despite our differing writing styles and healing approaches. Meeting in Mexico months later to fulfill this commitment, we challenged, confronted, and comforted each other whenever our personalities opted for chaos. No way could we convey the principles of soul empowerment without consecrating our lives to the practice of "essencing." Perhaps this is why the chapters sprang fully to life over a period of three months. Another possible reason for the accelerated birth is that we believed we made a soul agreement to write this book. A third is that our guides and teachers assisted us, reminding us daily that love connects dimensions.

We share this story simply to illustrate that no longer does success or growth happen only to someone "out there." We are all on this evolutionary journey together. It is an expedition involving no coincidences, though numerous opportunities to love one another. Love honors the sacredness of the soul. And it ensures that in collaborating with others we form irresistible spirals of multidimensionality that enhance the creativity inherent in each of us. In response, the universe applauds.

We thank you for being part of the journey. We wish you radiant health and prosperity in the course of remembering your magnificence. And we extend to you many blessings as you activate your multidimensional memory.

INTRODUCTION

Have you wondered why you are here? Do you feel fulfilled in your intimate relationships? Are you actively expressing your creativity? Do you experience a sense of purpose, power, and joy in your daily life? Are you low on energy, or suffering from a recurrent pain of unknown origin? Do your dreams point to the possibility of past lifetimes? Has your intuition been keeping you company? Do you have a sense that there must be something more?

We are all multidimensional beings who seek evolution. This quest has taken us through many lifetimes and numerous planes of existence. The everlasting part of us that desires wisdom is called **soul**, and the times and places through which it journeys constitute the **soul continuum**.

To learn the lessons of the physical plane—which include polarity, love, power, and discernment—we leave our **soul family** and come to earth in a physical body. At birth a veil descends, causing us to lose sight of our reason for coming. In the grip of this spiritual amnesia, we forget that we are multidimensional beings carrying within us the "spark of divinity." Memories of the abundant love and support we received from our soul family are also extinguished. With the passage of time, survival challenges posed by the earth plane further alienate us from our spiritual foundations. All the while the soul, with its twenty-four-hour-a-day guidance system, attempts to keep us aligned with our unique soul purpose.

It is as if, unbeknownst to us, we are enrolled in a carefully chosen educational program. Our soul purpose is our reason for incarnating; it defines the truths and values we will "major" in. Our life lessons—themes in which the soul needs more experience—form our "minor."

Most healing approaches focus on adjusting dysfunctional personality dynamics such as denial, resentment, fear, and shame. Once the majority of clients have broken through unhealthy patterns, however, learned limitations and adaptive behaviors deeply embedded in their consciousness will, like giant magnets, pull them back into dysfunctional behavior. Without the soul's support there is little chance to remain free in their own energy fields. To transform learned limitations and overcome addictions, personal will must be enfolded into divine will.

Lacking knowledge of their spiritual foundations, individuals see themselves as victims of circumstance, genetics, history, politics, or other external forces. When healers actively assist their clients in accessing the wisdom of the soul, on the other hand, an expanded scenario unfolds: conscious knowledge of their **soul agreements** infuses their lives with direction, continuity, and meaning.

The soul, which knows only truth, carries our distinctive cosmic blueprint. As such, the more adept we are at making choices aligned with our soul purpose and life lessons, the more likely we are to experience success and well-being. In fact, each time we intentionally activate the bylaws of our being, we mobilize enormous inner support for resolving and transforming personality issues. Exercising our capacity to link up with our soul's essence therefore accelerates not only our evolutionary progress but our creative expression and ability to manifest our desires on the earth plane.

Consider the expanded scenario. Imagine that at birth you emerged from a **spiritual context** teeming with guides and teachers, **past lifetimes**, and **soul affiliations**, into an existence imbued with a particular soul purpose and life lessons. To support you on your journey, you selected **soul qualities**—characteristics such as clarity, flexibility, and self-love—which, unlike personality traits, were resources associated with your soul purpose and life lessons. From infancy on, you were influenced by family, friends, school, religion, and the culture in which you grew up. In response, you developed a personality and a biography permeated with human content. Then, as time passed, you began consciously accessing your soul qualities, gradually enfolding your personal content into your spiritual context. In the end you simultaneously healed your personality issues and empowered your soul!

The movement from personal empowerment to soul empowerment is a passage from outer dictates to inner guidance, from attachment and possessiveness to reverence and joy. People who relinquish their learned limitations, vows of past lifetimes, and **psychic cords**, are free to honor their soul commitments. No longer crippled by energy blockages, they cultivate a respect for the body and its need for rest, play, love, and work; a sense of humor; a trust in inner guidance; enthusiasm for their chosen occupations; a capacity for surrender; an active expression of loving-kindness toward themselves, others, and the environment; knowledge of their unique form of creativity; a gift for affirming the divine in all people, events, and things; an appreciation for the interconnectedness of all life forms; and an ability to manifest their soul purpose, generosity, and a wisdom-based perspective.

This guidebook is designed to help you take the leap from personality to essence as you proceed toward healing yourself or others. In part 1 you will find a working vocabulary of soul attributes, together with examples showing how each one is expressed in the here-and-now and tips for becoming an agent in your own evolution. Part 2 describes ways to develop your consciousness and intuition—faculties that commune with the soul—as well as a step-by-step guide for conducting a soul reading and additional tools for accessing information. Parts 3 and 4 focus exclusively on the healing modalities of soul empowerment, culminating in an insider's views of the healing session itself.

The bulk of this work addresses various means of consciously accessing and developing the intuition. Why? Because the intuition affords quick and ready insights into the soul's cosmic report card, which evaluates our progress in understanding its purpose, its qualities, life lessons, placement on its continuum, and past lifetimes. The intuition also sheds light on the personality aspects in need of transformation. Although each person's intuition is as unique as a snowflake, you will have no difficulty introducing yours to the exercises and meditations presented. You will also have an opportunity to *experience* the formative role of intuition as you try out the healing techniques illustrated in part 4.

These techniques were perfected over thousands of sessions. Each one meets the following criteria: support to the soul, efficiency, simplicity, and effectiveness. Summaries of healing sessions have been included to demonstrate how the techniques may be applied.

Healing, you will discover, leads to the awareness that we are all multidimensional beings. The question then becomes: Are you willing to embrace your spaciousness and to explore your unlimited capacity for joy, creativity, and wisdom? If you are, prepare for a life-altering journey from personal empowerment to soul empowerment.

Part 1

LANDSCAPE OF THE SOUL

$\mathcal{O}ne$

THE SOUL CONTINUUM

. . . .

*"God became a human being in order that human beings
can become God."*

— Matthew Fox

S OME PEOPLE come to earth to acquire specific knowledge
for just a few lifetimes, while others choose earth as a school
and spend hundreds, if not thousands, of lifetimes here. Those
whose visits are sparse have opted to obtain learnings in other
dimensions. More frequent returns are the result of a number of
factors. In some instances, lessons are avoided for many lifetimes
before they are faced. In others, lessons are learned but more are
needed for the perfection and refinement of the soul purpose. In
still others, graduation is contingent on gaining mastery in a wide
range of subjects.

Every lifetime spent on the earth as well as time passed in
other dimensions constitutes part of a cycle which, once completed,
gives way to another cycle, all of which form the soul continuum.
Each cycle along the continuum has a theme, or soul purpose, and
every incarnation devoted to the theme moves toward increased
proficiency in that arena.

Each lifetime, too, has a motif of its own. In discovering yours,
you will have a lens through which to view your current challenges.
You will also see that every life you live influences all your future

lives. Sharing your clients' placement on the soul continuum will awaken similar revelations. Each of us, after all, is simply a moment in eternity!

The Lifetimes of Learning

All returns to the earth plane have a designated purpose in the soul's cycle of learning. Hence each one—from a practice lifetime to a completion lifetime—has unique characteristics.

Practice Lifetime

This lifetime is dedicated to discovery—to gaining awareness and experiences in a new arena. The only criteria for entry are sincerity and a willingness to practice a different way of being. Because this portion of the soul continuum often follows a completion lifetime geared to perfection, souls embarking on a practice lifetime tend to bring with them a penchant for high expectations. Here, however, there are no grades. Patience, compassion, and a sense of humor are recommended for one who has chosen to begin a new cycle of evolution.

Frank, in his early twenties, scheduled a session to explore his sexuality. He reported that he had many female friends yet had never been able to enjoy a healthy sexual relationship. When we asked for guidance, we were informed that Frank was in a practice lifetime learning about male consciousness. Furthermore, we discovered that he had chosen to embody as a woman in several previous lifetimes, during which he had completed his education in feminine ways of being and knowing. During many of these lifetimes as a woman, he had been devoted to religious and spiritual orders requiring celibacy. Hence he was accustomed to relating to women as sisters rather than lovers.

Frank mentioned that sometime in the past he had judged male energy. This lifetime, we learned, his soul had made a decision to learn about masculinity. He told us that everybody except him seemed to know the rules for being a man, and from a soul perspective, he was right! When we explained that he was in a practice lifetime, he breathed a sigh of relief. We assured him that he had done nothing wrong, that agreeing to be born into a male body was in fact an act of courage. We reminded him that he was under no obligation to exhibit perfect male consciousness.

Shirley, an educator in her late forties, requested our help in deciding about a career change. She was thinking about quitting her position as a team leader and beginning a private practice as a business consultant. She told us that she had longed to work with peers but was frustrated because her teaching colleagues seemed less creative and committed than she was. In reviewing her soul's history, we learned that she had already mastered working alone as a leader and was now in a practice lifetime to learn about *collaborative* leadership. Opening a private practice, we realized, would be comparable to auditing a course in which she had already achieved top honors!

Her challenge, as we saw it, was to overcome the pull toward reinvesting in previously mastered skills and begin grappling with the unfamiliar experiences of a practice lifetime. We encouraged her to explore collaborative leadership, rather than striking out on her own once again.

Return from a Soul-space Lifetime

At any point along the continuum, many individuals who have experienced a traumatic or exhausting lifetime on the earth plane choose to spend the equivalent of one or more lifetimes in soul space. While in absentia, taking time out from the rigorous curriculum, they gather strength and heal wounds.

Upon resuming their earthly lessons, these people tend to appear disoriented, and for good reason. Soul space is omniverse. Here, souls exist in a bodiless state of pure energy; living is holographic; and all information is readily available. There is no lapse between thinking and manifesting one's thoughts, and hence no need to approach life sequentially. Nor is there a need to learn, for everything is already known.

Fifteen-year-old Eric was referred to us because he was in danger of flunking out of school and was showing signs of depression. Although he understood the essence of his coursework, he had no concept of test-taking and little interest in completing his assignments. He was fascinated by the principles of physics, but could not understand why he had to take Algebra before enrolling in Physics. He often asked questions his teachers could not answer. They had labeled him a "troublemaker," and his friends called him a "show-off."

When we explained how we work, Eric said he was interested in exploring what was going on. Upon tuning in, we discovered that prior to his birth he had spent the equivalent of two lifetimes in soul space. As soon as we told him this, he groaned and burst into tears, saying he wanted to go back "home." We reminded him that nobody is drafted into duty on the earth and that his soul elected to be here.

He asked what his mission was, whereupon his guides explained that he had committed himself to translating the energetic principles he had learned in soul space. They reminded him that he experienced all information holographically and, as a result, found school boring. "You mean I'm not a stupid misfit!" he exclaimed, his face lighting up.

When we met with Eric's parents, we told them about his soul history and his soul purpose. His mother cried and said she had always known he was different. They then agreed to enroll him in a school capable of appreciating the workings of his mind.

Somersault Lifetime

To heal a split in consciousness, individuals will incarnate into circumstances diametrically opposed to those of a previous lifetime. They will go from monk to playboy, abuser to victim, warrior to peacemaker, extrovert to introvert, leader to follower, and vice versa. Having judged the opposing aspect of a polarity, they choose to make amends by exploring it. A return of this sort may occur more than once before a person moves on to an integration lifetime to fully heal the schism.

Terry, a poor, uneducated man in his early thirties, exhibited low self-esteem and described himself as a victim. We learned that in a past lifetime he had made a soul agreement to align with his personal power. In attempting to learn about the right use of will, he frequently overpowered others. He enjoyed being in control and welcomed any opportunity to demonstrate his prowess. At the end of that lifetime, he realized he had misused his power and decided to reincarnate as a person with no power. Both lifetimes were out of balance.

Linda, a ski-instructor in her mid-twenties, maintained few boundaries and behaved like an emotional sponge, picking up physical symptoms, fears, and frustrations from the people around her. When we asked for guidance about her placement on the soul continuum, we discovered a former lifetime in which she had been emotionally detached from others, priding herself on her independence and self-sufficiency. Her aloofness was legendary. For Linda, as for Terry, both lifetimes were out of balance.

Catch-up Lifetime

A catch-up incarnation often follows one or more practice or somersault lifetimes in which aspects of the soul purpose have been avoided. Concentration is centered on acquiring experience in these areas. (*Note:* Some degree of excess may be experienced in the course of aligning with the current soul purpose.)

Brian, a research assistant in his late fifties, had married someone he did not love in order to become part of a community. Not only was he dissatisfied with his marriage but he felt inauthentic in the community. As it turned out, he had spent several practice lifetimes learning to be a loyal member of a group. This lifetime his soul purpose was to explore individuation. He had a strong soul commitment to catch up on learning about his own needs, feelings, desires, and goals.

When we reminded him that he would receive no support from his soul for his loyalty to community, he replied, "I want to be true to myself without hurting anyone else, and I don't know how to do this." Every time he had considered taking action on his own behalf, he felt ashamed and overwhelmed with guilt. We assured him that others would not be offended by his decision to be more self-directed.

Theresa, a thirty-one-year-old advocate for people who are mentally challenged, was sensitive, empathic, and instinctively aware of people's needs. Serving others came naturally to her, but she had no idea how to pursue her own dreams, or even identify them. We found that she had dedicated several lifetimes to care-giving and that now her soul purpose was to catch up on establishing a sense of self-entitlement. Aware that she needed to follow her own yearnings, we advised her to delve into any subject that interested her and, if desired, study full-time.

Integration Lifetime

This lifetime is devoted to healing splits that occurred in previous lifetimes. It usually follows a number of incarnations in which the person led a dichotomous either-or existence. The current objective is to experience a "double major"—a dual focus that generates balance and peace. (*Note:* To appreciate the complexity of an integration lifetime, imagine what it would be like to enjoy two diametrically opposed loves at the same time!)

Joan, an attorney in her early forties, scheduled a session because she felt a sense of "unrelenting emptiness," even though she had a successful marriage, a prosperous career, and happy children. We discovered that she was in an integration lifetime and that her challenge was to combine her intuitive abilities with her well-developed intellect. Because others depended on her to be practical and analytical, she relied heavily on her intellect and did not trust her intuition. Learning that in past lifetimes she had sought refuge in her intuition, often at the expense of her intellect, gave her the hope she needed to begin harmonizing these two faculties.

Tracey, an entrepreneur in his late twenties, came to us because his life was "out of control." He felt like two different people, flipping between being the life of the party and withdrawing altogether from people and social events. While in solitude, he contemplated his role in life. When we asked for information about his placement on the soul continuum, we were not surprised to discover that he was in an integration lifetime and was being challenged to value both sides of his nature without judging either one.

Recovery Lifetime

This is a lifetime for healing addictions, traumas, or judgments made against oneself or others. Often a strong karmic pattern must be broken and released for the recovery to occur. Toward this end, people or events from past lifetimes may find their way into the present one. The keynote here is *intensity*.

Ruth, a music teacher in her late thirties, desperately wanted to be in a committed relationship and raise a family, but she questioned whether motherhood was actually in alignment with her soul purpose. Furthermore, although she instinctively knew she was a healer in hiding, any time she considered a career in healing, she had a panic attack and feared she would have to sacrifice something sacred to her.

When we tuned into Ruth's placement on the continuum, we discovered that she was in a recovery lifetime earmarked for overcoming previous trauma. During a past lifetime, she had been a well-known healer with three children who were seized from her because she refused to succumb to government edicts. Unable to locate her children through her psychic powers, she judged herself and fell into a depression. It became clear to us all that Ruth remained single, childless, and only partially committed to reclaiming her knowledge of healing so she could protect herself and her unborn children from an atrocity that occurred in the past. To recover, she forgave herself for failing to shelter her children in her previous lifetime. She also signed up for two classes in healing and deepened her involvement with a man she was dating.

Bill, an architect in his mid-fifties, had a history of broken commitments. Although he had initiated many projects, he never completed them. When we asked for guidance, we were not surprised to learn that in a previous lifetime his soul purpose was to dedicate himself to a religious order. Just before taking his final vows as a priest, he was called home because he was the only person available to tend to his dying mother and provide for the family. In answering this call, he abandoned his soul commitment to the priesthood.

We explained that in this lifetime whenever he was close to completing a project, he unconsciously sabotaged himself, never expecting to accomplish his goals. To heal, he agreed to "graduate" from the long-ago trauma and carry through with plans that made him happy.

Mastery Lifetime

This lifetime follows a series of existences focused on the same theme. Relative ease and clarity predominate, as long as the person remains aligned with the commitment to refinement, precision, and efficiency. Aspects of life that are not on the agenda to be mastered, however, can prove challenging.

Lee, a forty-two-year-old landscape artist, complained of a history of broken relationships and felt guilty for having less interest in his partners than in his art. His guides informed us that he had a soul commitment to become an acclaimed artist. He had majored in creative expression for many lifetimes, exploring the mediums of clay, color, fabric, even metals. When we reminded Lee that he was in a mastery lifetime, he held his stomach and laughed uproariously. We had given him permission, he said, to do what his heart demanded. We also urged him to give himself permission to attract a woman who would support his artistic endeavors.

Ingrid, in her late twenties, held a prominent position in a large corporation. Her male and female coworkers often told her they felt intimidated by her organizational competence. Although successful by all outward appearances, she felt stifled in this highly structured environment. Her true desire, we discovered, was to teach others how to use their creative talents. When we explained that she had made a commitment to a mastery lifetime in creativity, she smiled and acknowledged that the corporate setting did not support her creative expertise. She then decided to begin her own company.

Completion Lifetime

Qualities associated with a completion lifetime include a sense of urgency, perfectionistic tendencies, and incorporation of resources and learnings from many previous lifetimes. Equally apparent is an urge to clear up any karma that has accumulated. The potential for completion attracts people who remain unhealed or engaged in unfinished events. The good news is that upon successful completion, one has the choice of returning to earth to begin a new cycle on the soul continuum or going elsewhere in the universe to acquire other experiences.

Tom, in his mid-sixties, had recently retired from a successful business career. He had turned his attention to mentoring young people who were starting their own businesses; consulting on a volunteer basis with nonprofit community-oriented groups; and spending considerable amounts of time with his three grandchildren. Despite his ongoing accomplishments, however, he felt frustrated, unfulfilled, and in dire need of "contributing more."

Upon tuning into Tom's placement on the soul continuum, we discovered that he was in a completion lifetime and that he had made a commitment to consummate his many lifetimes of experience by teaching others. Excited that he was in alignment with his soul purpose, he quickly came to terms with his pressing desire to assist others, including his own grandchildren.

Ginger, an accountant in her early fifties, was unable to feel satisfied in her relationships even though she had attracted devoted partners throughout her adult life. After receiving information from her guides, we informed her that she was in a completion lifetime and had made a soul commitment to heal painful relationships of the past. She did not believe in past lifetimes, she confessed, though she had often felt as though her lovers were somehow familiar to her. We encouraged her to use this new information to exercise the healing potential within her existing relationships. We also reminded her to be gentle with herself and others.

Evolving Through a Cycle

Each lifetime spent diligently in a particular cycle increases the soul's mastery of that theme. A practice lifetime in a self-expression cycle, for example, will provide a bouquet of experiences in giving expression to the self. Later, an integration lifetime may be called upon to balance self-expression with the needs of a community, group, or family. During a completion lifetime, modes of self-expression will be perfected, refined, and perhaps taught to others.

Having evolved through the self-expression cycle, the soul is free to choose between returning to earth with a new purpose or serving in other dimensions. Volunteering for another cycle of earth-plane experience, it may select the theme of "service," or perhaps "power." It would then enter into a practice lifetime in the chosen cycle and thereby advance along the continuum.

To locate your placement on the soul continuum, begin by releasing any attachments you may have to the lifetime descriptions noted above. Then move into a state of unconditional thinking, often called "beginner's mind." Take a few gentle breaths and send out gratitude for already having the information about your placement. Ask your intuition for a simple yes-or-no response to the question "Am I in a practice lifetime?" Continue to ask about each of the lifetimes until you receive a "yes" that rings true. To challenge yourself further, inquire about the theme of the lifetime. Follow these guidelines when working with others as well.

In your search for answers, remember that all lifetimes on the soul continuum end at death—which ushers in a **past-life review**. At this point, the soul goes over its original cosmic report card and evaluates its progress. Depending on its desires for future growth and development, the soul chooses to either reincarnate on the earth or continue learning or serving in other dimensions. Decisions to reincarnate are accompanied by requests for a specific time, soul group or family, and even geographic location in which to incarnate. The past-life review concludes with a formulation of soul agreements.

Two

Soul Agreements

• •

*"When an inner situation is not made conscious
it happens outside as fate."*

—Carl Jung

PRIOR TO PHYSICAL incarnation, each individual enters into soul agreements with one or more people to further the evolutionary growth of all participating parties. The agreements are made on an individual, mutual, or group basis. These vows are more binding than contracts executed on the earth plane.

Learning the nature of your soul agreements will help you align the decisions you make with the bylaws of your being, and thereby become an active agent in your evolution. Uncovering the soul agreements of your clients will clarify many of their dilemmas and deepen their appreciation for the role they play in their evolution.

Individual Agreements

An individual agreement is formed when one person commits to incarnate in order to heal a particular aspect of a past lifetime. Although the issue to be healed may involve other individuals, they have no knowledge of the vow.

Robin, a celibate priest in a former lifetime, had been in love with a parishioner who was married. He never openly expressed his love, though he did write her reams of secret poetry. He also made a commitment to spend his next lifetime with her, although she made no such agreement with him.

At the time of his session, Robin was obsessed with the woman of his previous dreams, yet she rejected him because he was too intense. Only by breaking his original vow, as described in chapter 11, did he free himself to fall in love with a woman who loved him in return.

Mutual Agreements

A mutual agreement is formed when two people vow to incarnate together in order to complete unfinished business.

To heal their abandonment-betrayal cycle from a previous lifetime, Rachel and Beth had contracted to be together during their dying process this lifetime. Their agreement made no stipulation about who would die first; it merely arranged for the presence of both women while either one of them lay dying. The women were best friends throughout this lifetime until Beth developed breast cancer and went into isolation. Rachel, intuitively aware that her friend was dying, could not locate her and did not learn about her death until after the funeral.

Rachel blamed herself for failing to be with Beth during her dying process. Motivated by guilt, she decided to connect psychically with her friend's energy, and ended up merging with the part of Beth that had died of breast cancer.

During her session, Rachel acknowledged that Beth had reneged on her part of their soul agreement. We urged Rachel to break the vow that bound her to her guilt. Opting to continue taking full responsibility for having failed to help her dying friend, she refused, catapulting herself back into the familiar cycle of abandonment and betrayal. Two years later, Rachel developed breast cancer and died. Their mutual soul agreement, unfulfilled and unbroken, now tethers both women to their vow and the need for a return lifetime together.

GROUP AGREEMENTS

A group agreement is formed when several individuals vow to incarnate together for purposes of expanding upon or completing a work in progress.

Every summer, Rosalie volunteers eight days of teaching at the Creative Problem Solving Institute in Buffalo, New York, where she was once enrolled as a student. The first year she attended the institute, she recognized several of her teachers from previous lifetimes. Right away, soul agreements were remembered and honored. Rosalie and her former teachers, it turned out, had agreed to add their personal soul frequencies to further the evolution of the creative process. Now that many members of the original soul group reside in spirit, the agreement once again spans dimensions.

To uncover your soul agreements, try the *"freeze frame" technique*. It will open your cosmic photograph album containing agreements designed to further the growth and development of your soul. Begin by taking a few gentle breaths and quieting your mind. Then breathe into your heart and announce your readiness to access your soul agreements. Invite people you have known, whether they currently reside on the earth or in spirit, to parade in front of you. As each one takes form in your consciousness, reflect on the precise circumstances of your first meeting. Whenever an image corresponds with a freeze frame picture you have of the initial encounter, chances are that you share a destiny thread with that individual.

Each time a freeze frame experience is awakened, ask inwardly, "What is the exact nature of my soul agreement with _____?" Remember that some people will play the role of shadow-wisdom teacher, reminding you of your soul's truth by challenging you to express its opposite!

Be sure to review and update all soul agreements in light of your present soul purpose. Ask yourself, "In what ways does this agreement now serve the evolution of my soul?" Follow these guidelines while working with others too. As you do, remember that essence always seeks evolution.

Part 2

PATHWAYS TO THE SOUL

Three

CONSCIOUSNESS: THE WAY TO ALIGNMENT

●　●　●　●　●　●　●　●　●　●　●　●　●

"The ancestor to every action is thought."

—Ralph Waldo Emerson

I N EACH LIFETIME on earth, consciousness—which reflects the state of the soul—reminds us to one degree or another that we are spiritual beings learning how to be human beings. The more multidimensional our consciousness is, the better able we are to sustain this perspective and even align with the bylaws of our soul.

HUMAN NATURE -v- ESSENCE NATURE

As human beings, we are gifted with a human nature—composed of intelligence, emotions, a physical body, and a personality. The personality worries about trivialities, seeks approval, experiences emptiness, focuses on goals and results, and manipulates the self, others, and the environment. The personality also revels in drama, shame, and guilt, and succeeds in keeping us chained to our past through limiting beliefs.

Signs of being out of alignment with our human nature include the following:

- ◆ Disorientation
- ◆ Anxiety
- ◆ Emotional instability
- ◆ Lack of energy
- ◆ Illness
- ◆ Inability to follow through on commitments
- ◆ Absence of goals

As spiritual beings, we are gifted with a soul that connects us to past as well as future lifetimes, wisdom, a sense of universality, healing abilities, and creative potential. Signs that we are misaligned with our essence nature include these symptoms:

- ◆ Repetition of unhealthy patterns
- ◆ Confusion
- ◆ Lack of contact with guides and teachers
- ◆ Inability to access intuition
- ◆ Limited creative expression

In the best of circumstances, aligning with your human nature will not disrupt the alignment with your essence nature. At times, however, the personality—which identifies with security, separation, and scarcity—will demand one experience while the soul—which knows only wholeness and abundance—will want another. In such moments of tension, according to *A Course in Miracles,* the personality invariably speaks first, makes the most noise, and it is wrong. The good news is that the choice is yours: You can take action based on either your human impulses or your soul's desires.

To become more receptive to your soul's energies, you need only expand your consciousness of them. Just as reality has many dimensions, so does consciousness. People operating from different levels of consciousness, or vibrational frequencies, respond to the same event with different feelings and understandings. Yet the underlying truth is that we are always interacting with *all* the dimensions of reality, although we are not always aware of it. Any time you or a group you are working with needs a reminder, practice the Multidimensional Meditation on page 191 or the Group Multidimensional Being Meditation on page 192.

EXPANDING YOUR CONSCIOUSNESS

One way to expand your awareness is by taking charge of your thoughts. Attending to thoughts with focused intention redistributes energy, quickly lifting consciousness to a new level. Taking action at this point will prompt reality to mirror back to you this elevated state of consciousness. Mirroring occurs because the will, which is energy dependent, quickens when it is supported by intention and action.

Because thoughts emit vibrations, whatever you gift with your intention, you energize. If you focus on judgment, that is what will move toward you, raising a cloud of negativity in its wake. If you focus on love, you will attract the unifying force that heals all wounds. According to author Alan Cohen, every relationship, experience, and event in our lives is a reflection of the degree to which we are loving ourselves. If you want more love in your life, he advises, be more loving.

A second way to expand your consciousness is by releasing all limiting beliefs about relationships, finances, health, power, and career. To begin, think of areas in which you experience lack, resentment, or suffering. Then identify the belief you hold about yourself that attracts scarcity, ill will, or suffering. Finally, let it go.

As your commitment to soul empowerment strengthens and you begin approaching life with higher frequencies and expanded perspectives, additional limiting beliefs will arise to challenge you. This is a signal that you are on track. According to the principle of co-arising, *the more you align with your essence nature, the more any remaining aspects of your human nature that are misaligned with your essence nature will surface in order to be transformed.* Remember that all experiences of pain—whether they are physical, mental, emotional, or spiritual—express a resistance to your soul purpose.

Here is a list of common limiting beliefs:

"If I allow myself to be as competent as I know I am, I will risk being without a partner."

"It is selfish to take time for myself."

"I can't enjoy myself if anyone I love is in pain."

"I'd like nothing more than to be an artist (healer, teacher, volunteer), but I can't support myself doing what I love."

"If I do not take full responsibility for creating stability in my family, who will?"

"It's not safe for me to express myself."

"I know I need to make changes, but I can't bear to hurt anyone."

"I need to suffer in order to grow spiritually."

"I'll never meet anyone who will understand and love me."

"Women are not supposed to be ambitious (sexual, smart, powerful)."

"Men are not supposed to be sensitive (intuitive, expressive, loving)."

"I can't confront _____, because it might kill him."

"If I relax, I won't be able to earn enough money."

"If I love _____ enough, he will love me back."

"I'm too old to go back to school (divorce, remarry, confront my parents)."

"Happiness never lasts long."

"Because of my childhood, I'm a mess—and I'll never be any different."

"I can't help how I feel. I've always seen myself as less competent (beautiful, intelligent, creative) than others."

"I have to do all of it by myself."

TAPPING INTO THE ORGANIZING PRINCIPLES OF YOUR SOUL

Organizing principles are personal truths that guide our daily lives and give us a clear sense of purpose and meaning. They also serve to unify seemingly disparate events in our lives, thereby expanding our perspective. Another way to think about organizing principles is to envision them as soul values, or bylaws of our being.

To begin to recognize the organizing principles of your soul, reflect on the following questions: What are the soul-shaping events of your life? What have you always loved? What have you always known?

Personality, too, has organizing principles, some of which promote denial, struggle, and drama. Identifying your family of origin's organizing principles of personality will also help you clarify the organizing principles of your soul.

In Rosalie's family of origin, for example, the main organizing principles were duty and responsibility. For many years, she confused love (her soul's primary organizing principle) with duty and responsibility. In Michael's family of origin, fear and scarcity were organizing principles. He spent decades learning about healing and emotional balance (his organizing principles).

What were the principles exhibited by *your* parents? What role did these play in your development?

To go further in identifying your soul's organizing principles, follow these four steps:

1   List ten pivotal transition events in your life. Do not be concerned about whether the crossroads were positive or negative, chosen or circumstantial.

2   Invite your guides and teachers to assist you in accessing the deepest meaning underlying each of these events. Beneath every event on your list, record its meaning. Relax—this exercise is about allowing, not about judging or figuring out the answers.

3   Next to each event, name three people who supported you during the transition. Breathe deeply, then record the organizing principles they were supporting.

4   Observe how all these events conspired to reinforce and enhance your soul's organizing principles.

You have probably been actively moving toward the organizing principles of your soul all along. If so, be sure to acknowledge your progress. Perhaps give yourself a special name for having mastered each of the transition events on your journey. If you are in a creative mood, select one name that honors *all* the transitions.

Harmony, a sense of inner knowing, and joy will reflect evidence of your alignment with your soul's organizing principles. As you sustain this alignment, power, creativity, and wisdom will add to your sense of soul empowerment.

INTUITION: THE CHANNEL TO INNER GUIDANCE

"Every time we access multidimensional reality, we amplify our capacity to become manifestors of our own lives."

—Chris Griscom

I NTUITION FUNCTIONS like a walkie-talkie between the soul and the personality. A well-developed intuition is able to transmit and even amplify energetic impulses emanating from our essence nature. It can also intercept impulses coming from the essence nature of others. According to world-renowned psychic and healer Edgar Cayce, anyone interested in developing the intuition must create a union of mind, body, and spirit in order to use the self as a resource for the source. Lao-tzu, the ancient Chinese sage, advised aspiring channels to understand the masculine and keep to the feminine.

OPENING TO INNER GUIDANCE

Intuition, which often relays information through symbols, is experienced as a "felt sense of knowing." When we begin receiving messages from our intuition, our physical bodies respond with goose bumps—or "truth bumps"—flushed cheeks, and stirrings of the heart. As we become more familiar with these transmissions, the signs become more subtle; we may feel a soft touch on the cheek, a slight bristling of hair on the back of the neck, or a sense of warmth and well-being throughout the body. The more we act on the inner guidance of intuition, the more power, clarity, and purity we exhibit. According to author Shakti Gawain, each time we fail to follow our inner guidance, we feel a drop in energy, a loss of power, and a "spiritual deadness."

The quality and quantity of information received depends on the health of the emotional body. Why? Because the emotional body serves as the receiver, converting into information all incoming energetic impulses. The walkie-talkie's receiver, which is connected to the human body at the solar plexus, exists in the astral plane, outside of human time. As such, it is extremely sensitive and picks up frequencies from all dimensions.

People with a healthy emotional body can access the quickened frequencies of essence. Those who have not released and healed the trauma, anger, resentment, pain, or judgment clouding their emotional body cannot. For them, the information will lack clarity. It may also lack dimensionality, as the unhealed emotional body may be simultaneously converting impulses from the suppressed emotional energy.

When you ask for intuitive information, be sure to keep this point in mind. Also remember to shift your intellect to the passenger seat. The reason for moving the intellect into a secondary role is that it will try to analyze, edit, and interpret the inflow of information using only a small portion of consciousness; it is ill-equipped to connect with multidimensional energies. Its role is simply to sustain focused intention in order to give shape to the wealth of information coming your way. At the same time, do not disregard the role played by your intellect. Guidance received through your intuition without the support of your intellect may only diminish your life force and hurl you into a state of overwhelming confusion.

Inviting your intuition to lead and your intellect to support entails a constant questioning of old beliefs and conditioned thinking. To ease the transition, try imagining the body, with its intellect and intuition, as a vase holding the bouquet of spirit. As you come to rely more on your intuition, and support your inner knowing with your intellect, feelings and meanings will blend and will transmit their information holographically. From the perspective of the body as vase, there is no distinction between sensing information and knowing its meaning.

CONDUCTING AN INTUITIVE SOUL READING

One of Rosalie's favorite ways of using her intuition is by conducting soul readings. A soul reading is an energetic interpretation of an individual's psychospiritual development. It renders a blueprint of the person's soul purpose, soul qualities, life lessons, and personality aspects. The review concludes with insights to help further spiritual growth.

The prerequisites for conducting a soul reading are simple. For spirit to manifest, you will need to create a space filled with love, because the energy of love fosters cooperation between dimensions. To provide supportive mental activity, focus your thoughts on harmony. The blending of love and harmony will make your energy field irresistible to spirit. Finally, lead with your *enthusiasm,* or according to the original definition of the word, your excitement at being "filled with God."

The following sequence is recommended:

1 Relax body, mind, and emotions.

2 Focus on filling up with love.

3 Affirm. ("I am a resource for the source.")

4 Expand your energy field to merge with your client's.

5 Articulate the information you receive.

6 Consult with your guides for deeper meanings.

7 Extend gratitude to your guides.

Preparation

To engage your intuition, begin by relaxing. Experience all your cells, and the spaces between them, as smiling. Open your energy field by imagining two lines extending from the top of your head to your guides: one line for receiving information and the other for sending out gratitude. While continuing to relax, become inwardly attentive. (See the Relaxation Meditation on page 189.)

Focus your intention on filling up with love which, according to Saint Clare, is the source of all knowledge. Say yes to love as you inhale, and thank you to love as you exhale. Appreciate that your body instinctively knows the precise amount of energy to accept as you breathe in and to release as you breathe out. Give yourself permission to express your enthusiasm and to surrender to multidimensional consciousness. All the while, continue breathing deeply. Breath is the animation of love.

Affirm your intentions. Affirmations—I-statements expressed in positive terms—appeal to the subconscious mind. Remember, whatever you pay attention to, you become.

Examples of affirmations include the following:

"I am one with spirit and I enjoy my connection with the divine."

"I am a channel for God's love."

"With curiosity and delight, I welcome all conscious beings from all dimensions that are in alignment with my soul."

"I am a resource for the source."

Focus your intention on accessing divine truth effortlessly. Practice, not effort, will expand your consciousness and guarantee success. Remember that the transmissions are available to you twenty-four hours a day.

Energy follows thought. By affirming your willingness to be a channel for God's love, you become that channel! It is therefore important to maintain your self-confidence and appreciation for having this opportunity to serve. Judgments, comparisons, and feelings of unworthiness will only decrease your energy field. You are in charge of remaining present; spirit is in charge of presenting information and facilitating healing.

Expand your energy field to encompass your guides and teachers, as well as your soul affiliations in the devic, elemental, inner earth, angelic, and space realms (Refer to the Soul Affirmations Meditation on page 193). You will know these beings have come when you feel a change of energy in the room, or a distinct lightness of being. You will also experience a slowing down of your metabolism.

Once you have filled your energy field to overflowing, it is time to merge with your client as your beloved, as the most important person in the world to you at this moment. To merge your essence energy with that of your client, let your breath and intention move your energy in waves until it connects with the heart of your beloved. Affirm once more your delight in serving as a resource for the source. Then gently gift your client with your overflowing presence.

Essence responds to essence. Hence, when you intentionally merge with the essence of your client, her energy field will automatically open in greeting, like petals unfolding to receive the sun's light. As you surround your client with more and more love, her energy field will expand. Remember, to be recognized and received at the level of soul is what her energy field most deeply desires.

Energy from other dimensions is information on the earth plane. Therefore, everything you need to know about your client's soul purpose, soul qualities, life lessons, and even personality aspects will stream forth from her heart. Love, don't try. Focused intention is like a giant magnet that attracts the desired information; and in the process of intentionally accessing it, you will give it shape. As you do, remember to ground it in love and communicate it with compassion. (*Note:* Throughout the reading, remind yourself to breathe deeply. Breath facilitates the circulation of energy between dimensions.)

Accessing Soul Purpose

Ask your guides for information about your client's soul purpose. The moment you receive your first impression, sense, word, or "knowing," express it. Intuition is experienced to the degree that it is expressed. You do not need a wealth of information to begin. Simply say, "The first thing I am aware of is_____." Clarity will follow.

Information about your client's soul purpose will concentrate on the organizing principles of her soul. Aware of these principles, she will be able to make decisions and take actions that are in alignment with them. This is the information needed to promote direction, continuity, and meaning in her transition from personal empowerment to soul empowerment.

Examples of soul purposes include the following:

Communication: Self-expression, attunement to needs of self and others, expression of compassion toward self and others, sensitivity to dreams, writing, teaching, communicating with animals and plants, communicating with guides and other beings in different dimensions, communicating with spirit.

Emotional Development: Expression of the full range of emotions, emotional integrity, emotional balance, acknowledgment of emotional boundaries, discernment, flexibility, surrender of judgment, release of emotional rigidity.

Healing: Healing of self, healing of others, healing of animals, healing of plants, healing of the land, healing of the planet, attitudinal healing, past lifetime healing, use of prayer, energy work, music, colors, art, humor.

Individuation: Self-assertion, self-acceptance, trust in personal needs and desires and feelings, willingness to be visible, personal entitlement, creativity, goals, dreams, exploration of self, development and refinement of thinking.

Love: Self-love, love of others, forgiveness, sensuality, intimacy, sexuality, universal love, love of beauty, love of nature, love of country, love of truth, maternal love, paternal love, sibling love, love for a specific cause or calling.

Power: Right use of will, acknowledgment of choices, creativity, self-empowerment, collaborative empowerment, power through presence, political power, power to manifest desires and ideas, power in the world, power to create abundance, soul empowerment.

Service: Community service, religious service, planetary service, interdimensional service, generous offering of time and talents.

Accessing Soul Qualities

Now you are ready to receive information about your client's soul qualities, or "spiritual fingerprints." As always, ask your guides for assistance. A good way to understand these features is by imagining the sun as spirit and the rays of the sun as soul qualities, some of which your client agreed to individualize prior to her present incarnation.

Below is a partial list of soul qualities:

Abundance	Enthusiasm	Intuition	Self-esteem
Appreciation	Faith	Leadership	Self-expression
Balance	Flexibility	Learning	Self-love
Beauty	Focus	Love	Sensitivity
Celebration	Follow through	Loyalty	Service
Clarity	Forgiveness	Mindfulness	Simplicity
Collaboration	Freedom	Movement	Spontaneity
Communication	Generosity	Nurturance	Stability
Compassion	Gentleness	Openness	Strength
Confidence	Grace	Passion	Surrender
Contentment	Gratitude	Patience	Synthesis
Coordination	Harmony	Peace	Teaching
Courage	Healing	Perseverance	Thanksgiving
Creativity	Honesty	Playfulness	Transformation
Delight	Humor	Power	Trust
Discernment	Imagination	Purpose	Understanding
Discipline	Individuation	Receptivity	Visibility
Education	Initiative	Refinement	Vitality
Efficiency	Integrity	Release	Will
Empathy	Intelligence	Responsibility	Willingness

Accessing Life Lessons

Next, focus your intention on receiving information about your client's life lessons—the themes through which her soul seeks further growth and development. The information you provide will help her say yes to the motifs that add to her soul's evolution and no to those that add only to life's drama. The sustained alignment with your intuition gives rise to a delightful dance between being in the flow and translating its energy (information) with precision.

Life lessons appear in the following areas, among others:

Healing self-judgment
Overcoming silence and self-denial
Balancing support of self with support of others
Learning about the status quo
Practicing risk-taking
Replacing complexity with simplicity
Making self-determined choices
Delighting in being visible
Developing a leadership style
Trusting ease
Welcoming support on all levels
Healing relationships
Honoring spontaneity
Experiencing the benefits of practicality
Mastering grounded spirituality
Practicing collaboration
Learning about devotion
Seeking competence through career
Exploring unconditional loving or thinking
Following through on decisions
Discovering courage

Any time you do not understand the meaning of the information you receive, ask for more guidance, clarification, or elaboration. Avoid interpreting, judging, censoring, or embellishing. Go direct— ask your guides for assistance. Imagine that they are highly qualified consultants who will charge you $1 million each time you neglect to draw on their expertise!

Questions to your guides may be stated as simple queries requiring yes-or-no answers, or they may be more detailed, such as "What is the deeper meaning of this symbol (word, question, statement)?" or even "From what lifetime is this information coming?" Your guides, in turn, may present you with a picture that is personally meaningful to your client. If this occurs, be sure to describe the image to her, whether or not you understand its relevance.

While assisting a woman who was grieving the death of her eight-year-old daughter, Rosalie received the image of a bouquet of blue violets. In the process of describing the flowers to the woman, she began psychically receiving information about their meaning from the daughter, in the realm of spirit. Guides will often provide evidential information to verify the energetic presence of someone who no longer lives in this dimension. Had Rosalie attempted to add personal associations to the description of the flowers, she may never have known of the child's presence.

Also confer with your guides any time you are confused. Ask if you are picking up the confusion from your client or if it is yours. If it is yours, breathe in more love and refocus your intention. When Rosalie needs to entertain energies of a lighter frequency, she sometimes imagines a totem pole, then uses her breath and intention to move her consciousness farther up the pillar.

Remember that energy follows need, and that you are not in charge of determining the need. Occasionally, a past lifetime or soul agreement will surface to clarify a present-day challenge, or your client will benefit from understanding her placement on the soul continuum, or your guides may channel information from loved ones who reside in spirit. At other times you may experience a pause in the flow of information, or your client may need to rest before taking in more information. In such instances continue to send out gratitude, and trust the natural rhythm of the reading.

Accessing Personality Aspects

Only after elaborating on your client's soul qualities and life lessons should you seek information on her personality aspects. Personality serves as the body's survival mechanism. It is composed of knowledge, desires, behavior, and limited beliefs about oneself, others, and life in general.

Many personality aspects are in direct opposition to soul qualities and are therefore in need of transformation. For example, your client may have confusion as a personality aspect and clarity as a soul quality. Other polarities are inflexibility–flexibility and self-judgment–self-love. These negative correspondences arise in response to limiting beliefs imposed early in childhood. Consciously choosing to express the soul quality over the personality aspect will bring about the transformation needed to promote an alignment with one's essence nature.

A good way to identify your client's personality aspects is to ask yourself, "What lingering wounds express themselves as points of tension between this person's human nature and essence nature?" Then let your intuition guide you to the traits.

Here is a partial list of personality aspects:

Addictions	Lack of appreciation
Anger	Lack of compassion
Avoidance	Lack of confidence
Bitterness	Lack of creativity
Blame	Lack of generosity
Boredom	Lack of faith
Competitiveness	Lack of flexibility
Complaints	Lack of generosity
Confusion	Lack of humor
Control	Lack of joy
Defensiveness	Lack of patience
Dishonesty	Lack of power
Divisiveness	Lack of radiance
Doubt	Lack of self-confidence
Envy	Lack of spontaneity
Frustration	Lack of stability
Impatience	Lack of support
Insecurity	Lack of trust
Jealousy	Lack of vision
Sarcasm	Lack of vitality
Withholding	Lack of will

If in this portion of the reading your client requests specific information about health, relationships, or finances, first reconnect with her essence. Without taking this step, you may pick up on thought forms connected to her personality; and she may want so badly to hear a particular response that she will energetically project it, and that is what you will pick up. Always be sure the information you relay is channeled from her essence.

Remember, your role is not to please your client, but to serve as a representative of spirit. Impeccability is a must!

Conclusion

To end the reading, ask your client if she has any additional questions. If she does, answer them with the assistance of your guides. In response to some questions, you may receive no information, in which case it is acceptable to say, "I am receiving no information about that issue." It could be that your client's lesson is to learn from direct experience. In response to other questions, the information you receive may seem to answer a question different from the one you asked. It is best to convey the information as stated, without apologizing or filling in the blanks. The question may have prompted your guides to address an unspoken issue behind your request.

Next, check in with your guides one more time to be certain that all the information has been channeled. Take this moment of silence to send out gratitude to your helpers for having guided and grounded the reading, and ask that any resulting karma be neutralized. Then very gently withdraw your energy. Seal your energy field by repeating your telephone number, date of birth, or any other form of identification unique to you.

In closing, offer your client and yourself a big glass of water. After she leaves, you may want to wash your hands to symbolize that you are free in your own energy field once again.

FINE-TUNING YOUR INTUITION

During a reading, you will learn as much about yourself as you do about your client. Perhaps more than anything else, you will be able to assess your level of trust. You might recall moments in which you doubted your guidance, for example, and censored information your client needed to hear. Whispers of doubt are messengers reminding you to deepen your trust in the alliance you have with your guides, teachers, and soul affiliations. The more trusting you are, the more wisdom centered your channeled information will be.

To deepen your trust in your intuition, complete the following sentences:

My intuition was born the day that _____

I have most honored my intuition while _____

I rely on my intuition most when _____

The geographic regions that enhance my intuition are _____

The types of music that bring me closer to my intuition are _____

An intuitive dream I remember is _____

When I acknowledge that my intuition is the silent voice of spirit, I feel _____

When I imagine consciously accessing my intuition, I know _____

_____

I can count on _____ *to support my growing intuition.*

I consciously energize my own evolution by _____

To further develop your intuition, try these twelve exercises:

1   Essence seeks evolution. Imagining a clock, answer the following questions: What time is it in terms of your ability to relax your physical body? To quiet your mind? To be emotionally present? To trust your intuition?

2   Create a symbol to characterize relaxation of body, harmony of emotions, stillness of mind, and faith in intuition. Breathe the symbol into your heart and then into every cell of your body. It

will serve as your personal magic carpet to your intuition, spirit guides, and soul affiliations.

3   We are what we nourish most. Who are you?

4   What are your most cherished truths? With whom do you share them? How do you celebrate them?

5   In what ways would your life be different if you allowed yourself to feel more peaceful, purposeful, and powerful?

6   Who are the teachers of your spirit? How have you incorporated their teachings into your life?

7   What inspires you?

8   Reflect on an uncomfortable situation with which you are currently grappling. Ask yourself, "What belief about myself could have created these circumstances?" Then breathe deeply and ask yourself for the most evolved expression of that belief.

9   Recall an idea, feeling, dream, or vision you have recently had. Ask yourself, "Does this perception serve my essence or my personality?" If it serves your personality, ask yourself, "How do I progress from a perception of separation or lack to one that embraces essence?"

10   Complete these two statements. "I am essential to the evolution of the planet because _____.

I therefore vow to _____."

11   Over the course of the next seven days keep a record of the choices you make, beginning a new page each day. At the end of the day, decide which choices nourished your soul and which ones nourished your personality. Look for patterns. Determine areas in which different choices would have been more helpful. End each page with: "I affirm _____."

12   For one month, keep a diary of how you have added to the love in the world.

Additional Techniques for Tracking Information

> "The laws of ecology are the laws of energy. Everything
> is interconnected; every atom, every movement
> of the focus changes the universe."
>
> —Starhawk

IN MOVING from personality empowerment to soul empowerment, two additional techniques—Neuro-Linguistic Programming and Kinesiology—can be used to support your intuition. They may also be used on their own while you develop your intuitive capacities.

In both instances they are likely to be as healing as they are informative. When we started working with clients, for example, we would blend our energy with theirs to sense where their blockages were. At times, unable to clear their energy from our bodies, we ended up with some of their aches and pains. After learning Neuro-Linguistic Programming and Kinesiology, we were able to track the energy of our clients without becoming energetically stuck ourselves.

Neuro-Linguistic Programming will help you enhance your self-understanding. In addition, it will help you track a client's mode of accessing, processing, storing, and retrieving information; confirm your intuition; decide on possible next steps to take; and keep your energy field clear. Kinesiology, applied to your energy field or your clients', will assist you in determining whether it is strengthened or weakened by a particular object, relationship, thought, or substance—such as an herb, homeopathic remedy, or other medication.

Neuro-Linguistic Programming (nlp)

Throughout infancy, we take in information through six sensory pathways: our eyes (visual), ears (auditory), touch (kinesthetic), mouth (taste), nose (smell), and intuition (psychic). By the time we start school, most of us have developed one preferred pathway of communication. The senses used most frequently in today's population are sight, hearing, and touch, or feelings. These are the three channels addressed by NLP, a method designed to track and interpret how a person is interacting with the environment.

NLP reveals the many challenges involved in communicating. The majority of them hinge on the fact that people are most comfortable working with those who communicate through the same channel they do. In fact, mismatched channels is one of the key culprits in relationship struggles, learning difficulties at school, and conflict on the job. Problems persist because few partners, teachers, or managers are skilled in communicating equally well on all three channels. To effectively heal ourselves and others, we must take note of these findings and expand our awareness to embrace the fact that other people make sense of the world in ways we do not.

The Three Orientations

Visual people receive and process information by seeing and creating mental pictures. Typically, they will use such phrases as "*Show* me," "*See*," "It *looks* like—" or "*Watch* this." When confused, they may say, "I just can't *see* it." The majority of top business executives, architects, and engineers are visual.

Auditory people receive and process information by hearing words and sounds. They tend to use such phrases as "*Tell* me," "It *sounds* like—" and "I'd like to *hear* more about it." When puzzled, they are apt to say, "That doesn't *sound* right" or "I just can't *hear* you." Many English teachers, musicians, and poets are auditory.

Kinesthetic people receive and process information through feelings and sensations. They are apt to say, "It *feels* like—" "It *feels* good to me," and "I have a *sense* you want me to—" When perplexed, they may tell you, "Something doesn't *feel* right" or "I just can't *feel* it." Many artists and sculptors are kinesthetic.

In a safe, relaxed environment, people are willing to use a non-primary channel of communication. If conflict arises, however, they will revert to their dominant mode. Lovers immersed in an exchange of feelings, for example, will respond to discord by retreating to their more highly developed sensory pathways. "I need you to *tell* me you love me," one may say. "I need to *hear* the *words!*" (auditory). The other may respond with, "I *show* you I love you by— Why can't you *see* that I love you?" (visual). Although they care about each other, neither one is communicating in a way that the other can clearly understand. Their verbal volley will invariably peak in frustration, a signal that they are operating on different channels.

The affinity for a particular set of words is not the only difference between the three modes of interacting. Visual people often speak at a fast clip in a high-pitched voice. They need to "see the picture." You can give them verbal directions forever, to no avail. If you start describing your feelings, they will get bored or confused. If you draw them a picture or hand them a map, however, they will glance at it and turn away satisfied. With the picture in their minds, they will have all the information they need.

Auditory people usually speak in more moderate, medium-paced tones, emphasizing resonant effects and verbal descriptions. Detailed pictures and feeling states have little meaning for them. To truly comprehend a situation, they need words and sounds.

Kinesthetic people often speak in a soft, low-pitched, slow-paced voice, all the while feeling the meaning of their words. Lightly touching them on the arm will let them know they are understood. To make sense of their world, they need to experience its texture.

Interpreting Eye Movements

In the early 1970s Richard Bandler and John Grinder, the founders of NLP, discovered a link between eye movements and brain activity. Using the horizontal plane of the eyes as a frame of reference, they found that a person whose eyes move upward is processing information visually; a person whose eyes remain level with the plane is hearing words and sounds, and is processing information via the auditory channel; and a person whose eyes drop below this plane is processing information kinesthetically.

While facing a person and noting his eye movements, you can use these clues to identify his preferred channel of communication. You can also determine whether he is recalling a past experience or constructing new information. Using the vertical plane of the nose as a frame of reference, observe his eyes. If they move to the right of this plane (the observer's right), he is recalling a memory. An easy way to remember this association is to equate the *r* in *right* with the *r* in *recall* (right = recall). If the person's eyes shift to the left (the observer's left), he is constructing new information (left = construct).

This cue, although significant on both the visual and auditory channels, is particularly revealing on the kinesthetic level. A person who is looking down to your left is experiencing an emotion in the present.

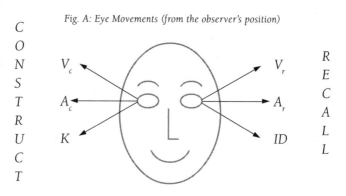

Fig. A: Eye Movements (from the observer's position)

V = Visual: A = Auditory; ID = Internal dialogue; K = Kinesthetic;

Subscript R = Recall; Subscript C = Construct

A person who is looking down to your right is searching for the "correct" feeling to express, based on prior experiences, and is engaging in internal dialogue.

Internal dialogue is rooted in past programming. Many people raised by strong authority figures have had little opportunity to develop a sense of their own feelings. When they are in internal dialogue they are searching for the feelings with which they were programmed to respond. It is safe to assume that an individual who is looking down to your right is embarking on a downward negative-energy spiral leading to confusion, negativity, and depression. If he is looking straight down, he may be feeling shame.

Fig. B: Dissociation and Shame

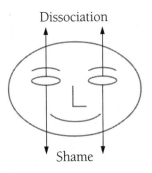

Two additional eye positions are worth noting. In one, the eyes are unfocused and staring straight ahead in the auditory position. Staring is associated with daydreaming, and indicates that the person is visually or psychically seeing a picture. In the other position, the eyes go straight up. This usually occurs when people are starting to feel intense emotions and are on the verge of tears. Although close to a breakthrough, they have become scared of feeling their pain and look upward to both avoid their feelings and hold back their tears. Splitting off from one's feelings to avoid reexperiencing a past trauma can indicate a state of dissociation.

Here are some additional points to keep in mind:

1 When using NLP to observe yourself, remember to reverse the left-right positions. In this instance left = recall and right = construct.

2 NLP tracking holds true whether you are right- or left-handed.

3 The alleged shifty-eyed person whose eyes spin from side to side may in fact be an auditory individual who is having a conversation with himself.

4 The only times we have experienced people changing their preferred channel is after healing past traumatic experiences or after being educated in NLP.

5 Because each channel distinguishes itself through the use of a different set of words, inflections, tones, pitches, and verbal speeds, NLP can be used when you have no visual contact with the person, such as on the telephone.

Skill-Building Exercises

Two of the following exercises require the use of a partner. Practice with someone you are comfortable talking to—a colleague, a friend, or your significant other. All three exercises can be performed in a group setting.

Observing Eye Movements—The objective of this exercise is to gain experience in observing eye movements so you can discover how people are accessing information. To begin, sit directly across from your partner, relax, and decide which one of you will be the first speaker. The speaker may address one of the "suggested topics" listed below or a subject of her own choosing.

The first speaker starts by talking for 3 to 5 minutes. The listener mentally notes the speaker's words, phrases, and eye movements. The listener uses active listening and does not interrupt with questions or reactions. Writing down the dominant communication pattern and other observations is permissible, provided that the speaker will not feel self-conscious. Then reverse roles and repeat these steps.

Referring to the "review" listed below, discuss what you each saw, heard, and felt. (In a group setting, repeat this exercise with at least two other partners.)

Suggested Topics

Describe the home and neighborhood in which you grew up.
Describe your first love.
Describe the first car you owned.
Describe your favorite restaurant.
Describe the best vacation you ever had.
Describe a memorable learning experience.

Review

Which eye movements did you observe?
What key words were used?
How many channels were used?
What was your partner's dominant channel?
What was your partner's secondary channel?
What else did you notice?

Also pay attention to the eye movements and key words used by friends, family, business associates, even strangers. The more you practice, the more skilled you will be.

Bridging—To deepen your rapport with someone who communicates on a different channel, you can match the person's words, tone, and verbal speed, but it is extremely difficult to do so for long periods of time. Besides, it is as important to honor your own preferred channel as it is to honor another's. A healthy compromise is to "bridge" your communication style with the other person's by combining the vocabulary, tones, and speeds of both channels.

The purpose of this exercise is to practice bridging your communication style with others'. Allow 3 to 5 minutes per person.

Sit facing your partner and each state your strongest channel. (If you both have the same primary channel, be sure that one of you switches to a backup channel.) Decide who will speak first. The speaker begins by talking about a hobby or special interest. The listener participates in the conversation via "bridging statements" similar to those listed below. Then reverse roles. (In a group setting, repeat this exercise with at least two other people whose preferred channels are different from your own.)

Bridging Statements

◆ **Visual to auditory**: "I can really *hear* what you are saying. Before, the *picture* I had was incomplete."

◆ **Visual to kinesthetic:** "I was *seeing* it another way. Now that you have shared your *feelings* and concerns with me, I have a different *sense* of what you're up to."

◆ **Auditory to visual**: "Your *words* are so precise that I can clearly *picture* what you are saying."

◆ **Auditory to kinesthetic**: "I can *feel* your sincerity, and it *sounds* as though I need to rethink the project."

◆ **Kinesthetic to visual**: "It *feels* like the *image* you are presenting is wonderful."

◆ **Kinesthetic to auditory**: "*Sounds* great! Those *words* give me a real *feel* for your passion."

Practice bridging communication channels with friends, family, and business associates. The more you practice, the more versatile you will be.

Experiencing Internal Dialogue and Authentic Feelings—This exercise will transport you from the obstructed emotions of internal dialogue into present-day feeling states. Learning to initiate this shift will help you break through impasses in intrapersonal communication.

Standing alone, place most of your weight on your left foot, tilt your head diagonally down to the left, and focus on a spot about 18 inches (45 cm) to the left of and the same distance in front of your weight-bearing foot. Now relax and fully experience all your feelings. After a few minutes, record your experiences on paper. (Did you feel uncomfortable, shaky, sick, heavy, dark, or negative? Did you feel as though authority figures of the past were trying to dominate you?)

Reverse your position, placing most of your weight on your right foot and tilting your head diagonally down to the right. Look at a spot about 18 inches (45 cm) to the right of and the same distance in front of your weight-bearing foot. Again relax and fully experience your feelings. After a few minutes, record these experiences. (Did you feel lighter, clearer, happier, and perhaps freer?) When this exercise is performed in a group setting, many participants note that the energy in the room becomes lighter. (When working with others, be sure to end with the second position, so no one is left in internal dialogue!)

If you felt uneasy in the second position, chances are that you were discouraged from developing your feelings as a child. If emotions are in fact alien to you, then internal dialogue—echoes of your past programming by authority figures—is all you know. It will take practice to feel comfortable with your authentic feelings. To develop this channel of communication, tell yourself, "Putting my weight on my right foot and looking down diagonally to my right is the right thing to do!" Then do it, several times a day.

NLP As a Healing Technique

NLP can be used to access unconscious information, resolve trauma, and reprogram the mind with positive information. To initiate your own healing, first identify your preferred channel of communication. Then ask yourself, "Have I shut down my other channels?" If the answer is yes, ask yourself how old you were at the time and what caused the shutdown. If you are a healer, NLP will help you discover how your clients process information, bridge your communication style with theirs, and track channels that may need to be cleared.

Resolving Present-life Trauma—Any time pain or fear becomes too much to bear, it can overload the nervous system. To stay alive, the individual may have to shut down one or more sensory channels. Witnessing an accident involving a loved one or a pet, for example, or seeing one's parents fighting violently, may shut down the visual channel in order to block access to the painful pictures. Hearing the screams of a loved one who cannot be reached, listening to parents fighting, or being verbally abused may close off the auditory channel. Sexual abuse, beatings, or other trauma to the feelings may block off the kinesthetic channel. Following exposure to prolonged abuse or torture, an individual may shut down all sensory channels and dissociate from his body.

Regardless of how mild or extreme a trauma is, all memories of the event remain locked in the subconscious mind. With the help of NLP, these events can be identified and reexperienced through the same sensory pathways that were originally affected. As details of the trauma begin to surface in conversation, the buried pictures, sounds, or feelings emerge into consciousness—much like the air that escapes after sticking a pin into an inflated balloon. With the release of the blocked energy, the closed channels reopen, initiating an increased energy flow that activates the body's healing process.

Resolving Past-life Trauma—Over the centuries, numerous people have shut down their visual channels after seeing their loved ones tortured or killed, their villages destroyed, or other horrifying spectacles. Some went so far as to gouge out their eyes so they could not see. Destruction of the auditory and kinesthetic channels was also common.

People who were not healed of their traumas brought them forward. Indeed, individuals born into this lifetime with soul commitments to clear their unresolved traumas will energetically recreate similar events in order to do so. Simply put, people carry trauma until it is healed—or, more accurately, trauma keeps coming up, seeking to be healed.

NLP works equally well in these instances. The eye positions indicating past-life sensory shutdowns are identical to those associated with shutdowns in this lifetime.

Reprogramming the Mind—After any release, the empty spaces within the person's energy field must be filled with positive frequencies. His soul essence, the return of his soul qualities, as well as positive statements and affirmations will all enhance his energy field. Aware of his preferred NLP channel, you will be able to deliver this positive energy in the communication style he is most likely to accept. His conscious mind will then allow the information to flow unobstructed into his subconscious mind. His super-conscious mind, if already activated through an opening prayer, will assist in the integration.

Be sure to incorporate NLP into your healing sessions. Here are a few pointers to help you make the most effective use of this technique.

Positioning Yourself—The path of least resistance and greatest impact is the one leading through the feelings. For this reason, you will want to sit slightly lower and to the left (the healer's left) of your client. This position will naturally encourage him to access his feelings (kinesthetic) as he interacts with you.

Opening the Session—Begin by asking your client why he made the appointment and what he would like to change or heal. Then inquire about when the dilemma began and what part of his body it affects. As he speaks, pay attention to his eye movements and speech patterns, as well as the tone and pitch of his voice. In phrasing subsequent questions, match your client's preferred channel.

Allowing for the Recollection and Integration of Information—Any time your client's eyes go to a recall or construct position, remain silent and hold the love vibration for him. (The only exception to this rule is when your client is in internal dialogue or dissociation, which are discussed below.) In recall mode, he may be bringing to awareness a past trauma that has been locked away in his subconscious mind. Breaking this link can cause the memories to slip back into the depths of his subconscious. In construct mode, he may be integrating new information received during a breakthrough. Interrupting at this point will only rob him of an opportunity for healing.

Your task is to patiently allow for the completion of the process. Wait for your client to clearly indicate—by taking a deep breath, sighing, or returning his attention to you—that he has completed the search or integration. Then softly ask if he needs more time or if he is ready to continue. When in doubt, sustain the pause.

Attending to Internal Dialogue—If your client slips into internal dialogue, get him out of this channel as quickly as possible. Divert his attention with questions, such as "Who were you just talking to?" "What were you remembering?" "What were you just experiencing?" or "Where did you just go?" Once you have the information, gently ask him to "come back" and look at you.

If your client keeps slipping into internal dialogue, firmly demand, "Get out of there!" In a group situation, do not hesitate to call out across the room, "Bill, stay with us!"

Your goal is to break up the internal dialogue. Why? Because the longer your client remains connected with his past programming, the further away he will drift from his true feelings, and the greater his risk of energy loss and depression. Your goal is also to pay attention to themes that trigger an internal dialogue, for they can clue you in to the nature of the programming, as well as the ways in which it manifests in your client's life. With this information, you will be able to uncover and release obstructed emotions.

Coping with Dissociation—In instances of dissociation you have even less time to intervene. Whenever your client stares straight upward, have him lower his eyes *immediately* to avoid splitting off from his feelings. Refrain from asking questions, which will only encourage him to escape into his head. Instead, firmly tell him to look at you, breathe into the pain, and exhale through it. Be prepared—he may burst into tears as he breaks through the trauma!

Breakthroughs Achieved through NLP

In an opening prayer during a recent introductory lecture, we mentioned that some people can see energy, others can hear it, and still others can sense or smell it. Suddenly, one of the women in the room jumped up excitedly. She explained that she had "just heard energy for the first time." Apparently, our prayer had given her permission to hear the sound frequencies in her midst.

Sally, at age thirty-nine, exhibited signs suggesting that she may have been sexually abused as a child. She refused to look us directly in the eye, declared that she did not feel safe around men, said she was unable to sustain a relationship with a man, and was overweight. We asked her if she would be willing to do an experiment, and she agreed.

We had Sally take a deep breath and relax. We then explained that we were going to ask her a question and invite her to feel the answer in her body. When we sensed that she was calm and centered, Rosalie asked her in a soft, calm voice, "Sally, as a child, were you sexually abused?" Immediately her eyes went to visual recall and her facial muscles tightened. She admitted that she had indeed been sexually abused and had kept it secret all her life. We proceeded to help her release her pain, shame, and guilt, as well as the energetic imprint of the abuse.

Normally, in response to a question of this nature, there is either no physical reaction, which we interpret as a "no," or one strongly suggestive of a "yes." If a client's eyes go to visual recall (up and to our right), we know she is seeing a picture of something that happened in her past; if her eyes go to auditory recall (eye level and to our right), she is hearing something; if they go to kinesthetic (down and to our left), she is tapping into her feelings; if they go to internal dialogue (down and to our right), she is remembering past programming. In each case, we seek further information by softly asking direct questions, such as "What were you seeing? What was the picture you just saw?" or "What were you hearing? Who were you just talking to? What did they say?" or "What are you feeling?" or "How do they want you to act?" These sensory-based questions help open the pathways to blocked memories and facilitate their release.

Christine, a teacher in her early thirties, was participating in a workshop. When the group paired off to do NLP eye-watching exercises, her partner expressed confusion, because her eyes never went to recall. After about fifteen minutes of trying to elicit information about her childhood, including anything that may have caused her to lock away her memories, our intuitions told us to back off. We explained to her and to the group that we could not pinpoint why this was happening and that it would be best to move on.

As we began discussing the next subject, Christine interrupted with the news that she could remember suffering a nervous breakdown as a teenager and vowing to keep this memory buried deep within her unconscious, for fear of triggering another breakdown. While speaking, she allowed herself to cry. From that moment on, she shifted easily into visual and auditory recall, and had no trouble accessing her memories.

KINESIOLOGY

Kinesiology, also known as muscle testing, is used to determine the energetic effect of various agents on the human body at a particular moment in time. This technique works well for testing the body's response to individual foods, vitamins, herbs, homeopathic remedies, items of jewelry, crystals, even thoughts, beliefs, and relationships. If you are deciding between several options, it can let you know the one that is most strengthening to your body or another's.

The principle behind Kinesiology is that energy influences energy. Surrounding each person, animal, plant, and mineral is a sensitive energy field called an aura. In a person, this subtle auric field is energetically responsive to everything he eats, drinks, thinks, and wears. Eating well, drinking pure water, thinking uplifting thoughts, exercising appropriately, and wearing colors and jewelry that enhance a person's auric field will strengthen his physical body.

How to Muscle Test

For this, you will need a partner and an object to test. Have your partner stand facing you, with her feet a shoulder-width apart and her eyes relaxed and looking straight ahead. Ask her to raise her writing arm out to the side and make a fist. Advise her to keep her arm as rigid as possible and to refrain from moving it upward as you work.

Begin by testing the relative strength of her arm. Pressing downward on her wrist or forearm with your strongest hand, tell her, "Resist, resist, resist." Note the strength of her resistance.

Allow your partner to rest for a moment. Then have her stand in front of you in the same position as before. Place the object to be tested in her free hand, and ask her to hold it in front of her heart. Once again, muscle test. Is her arm stronger, weaker, or the same as before? A stronger arm implies that the object is enhancing the person's energy field, whereas a weaker arm indicates that the energy field has been compromised. An arm that remains the same suggests that the object is having little energetic impact.

If your partner tests strong, you may continue testing other items. If she tests weak, advise her to shake off the new energy and take a moment to rest; then test her *without* the object to make sure she has regained her strength. Once you have confirmed her strength, she will be ready for further testing if desired.

To determine the effects of thoughts, beliefs, or relationships, muscle test your partner's responses to yes-or-no questions. Have her stand normally, with her writing arm out to the side. Ask her body for a "yes" response, noting whether her arm remains the same or becomes stronger; then test for a "no" response, checking to see if the arm weakens. Once you have the reference points you need, proceed by asking your partner to concentrate on a particular thought, belief, or relationship. Test her outstretched arm as you ask her body yes-or-no questions such as "Is this new job aligned with your essence?" "Is your relationship with _____ supportive of your essence?" or "Is working with (name of healer) congruent with your soul's organizing principles?" Be sure to ask only one question at a time, allowing your partner to shake off any negative energy before continuing.

Reversing positions, have your partner test you. Perhaps you would like to learn about your past lives and where you are on your evolutionary path. If so, your partner would muscle test your body's responses to such questions as "Do you have a soul affiliation with the angelic (devic, elemental, inner earth, space) realms?" "Where are you on the soul continuum? Are you in a practice (return from soul-space, catch-up, integration, recovery, mastery, completion) lifetime?" "Do you have a soul agreement with _____ ?" and "Is the decision to _____ in alignment with your soul purpose?"

Although Kinesiology is a useful adjunct to soul readings and NLP, its applications are somewhat limited. For one thing, an outstretched arm will tire fairly quickly, hence only a certain amount of testing can be conducted at any one time. For another, muscle testing restricts the amount of interactive dialogue you can have with your client.

Sue, a nurse in her late thirties, arrived wearing a fabric ankle bracelet. She told us it was a gift from her boyfriend. We asked if she would like to test it. Right away, she removed it and we tested it—only to find that it weakened her. We were guided to ask her if in a past lifetime she was a slave-girl to the man who was now her boyfriend. She held her breath, lowered her eyes to the shame position, and complained of a knot in her stomach—signals we interpreted as a "yes" response from her body. She then explained that whenever she wore the ankle bracelet she and her boyfriend seemed to fight more.

Sue forgave him for his controlling behavior in their previous incarnation together. At this point, the ankle bracelet tested neutral. Even so, we saw no positive gain from putting it back on and too many potentially negative consequences. We advised her to refrain from wearing it.

Carl, a manager in his late forties, wore a large metallic medallion around his neck. When we asked why he wore it, he said he liked it and believed that it strengthened him. He agreed to let us muscle test it. As we tested the medallion, his arm weakened considerably.

We then asked if he had worn a similar medallion as a warrior in another lifetime. His intuition told him he had. We asked if he was kind and loving in that lifetime. His intuition told him he was not. When we asked if he was ready to forgive himself, he said yes. After he cleared the energy, the medallion tested neutral. All the same, we strongly suggested that he not wear it for a while, or better yet, that he consider giving it away because of its potentially negative consequences.

Steve, a musician in his late twenties, felt challenged by intimacy. He told us that when he was a young teenager his divorced mother gave him her wedding band to wear, asking him to promise always to be hers. Steve wore the ring without questioning its effect on him. We confirmed through muscle testing that the ring weakened him. After the session, Steve met with his mother and, breaking his promise to her, removed the ring.

Inga, an astrologer in her late thirties, wished to test a quartz crystal she wore to ground herself. When tested, it showed that it in fact weakened her. After helping her clear her fears about being on the earth and abusing her power—concerns related to harm she had inflicted in previous lifetimes—we retested the crystal. This time it strengthened her. Because it had a positive effect on her, we were certain that her fears had caused it to test negative. As these were now cleared, we recommended that she continue to wear the crystal.

It is interesting to note that personal items producing negative responses will test positive after their wearers release their trauma. The reason for the reversal is this: As our negative thoughts and beliefs are released, our consciousness changes and so do our physical responses.

READING BODY SIGNALS

* *

*"Feelings repressed in childhood retain their potency and influence
our body and mind often for the rest of our lives."*

—Alice Miller

IN MULTIDIMENSIONAL HEALING, reading the body's
signals is as important as listening to words. The physical body
provides valuable information about the issues with which a
person is grappling. The emotional body, its energetic "glove," can
be equally revealing.

MESSAGES FROM THE PHYSICAL BODY

The physical body carries memories of all past events in the soul's
evolution. It also holds the keys for unlocking every one of them,
including those that contribute to our innermost dilemmas.

Signals Encoded in the Body Structure

Built into the structure of the physical body are clues about past-
life endeavors and present challenges. Large-boned people with wide
shoulders, a stocky build, and a short, broad neck were often
warriors in other lifetimes. A person with this body type may be
working through issues of power, trust, feeling safe, letting go of
control, or learning to love.

People with more rigid, thinner, and somewhat emaciated bodies were more likely monks, nuns, or members of other religious orders. They appear solemn and sullen, and tend to seek solitude. More often than not, they are carrying forward unresolved effects of poverty, celibacy, pain, suffering, and denial of bodily needs. A person with this body type may be working through issues of self-love, speaking out, visibility, creativity, or claiming personal power.

Many people with a long, skinny neck, finely chiseled fingers, and a propensity for sophisticated manners, dress, and thoughts have spent lifetimes as members of a privileged class. Now they may be learning about opening their hearts and letting go of an inflated sense of entitlement. Numerous people who are overweight were deprived of food or starved to death in other lifetimes, or were sexually abused in this lifetime. The challenge for people with this body type is to articulate their anger, resentment, and pain.

Maria, a geneticist in her late fifties, was scheduled for back surgery, which she was afraid she would not survive. Since her teenage years, she had suffered from recurring backaches as well as psoriasis on her hands. Reading her body structure left us with no doubt that she had been a mighty warrior in past lifetimes; her frame was powerful and stocky. Her voice and demeanor, however, were exceedingly gentle and kind. As we tuned into her energy, we sensed that she had participated in a horrible battle, after which she had judged herself and cursed her hands as they dripped with blood.

After helping Maria break the vows of past lifetimes, we had her look at her hands and forgive them for all the killing they had done. We then asked her to send them unconditional love. Before our eyes, the scaly patches on her hands lost their redness and began to heal. By the end of the session, her back pain had vanished and she knew that if she still needed the operation she would be fine.

Ken, a carpenter in his late forties, was having a hard time earning enough money to support his family. He also felt guilty about being married. Observing Ken's thin, almost stiff body structure, we surmised that he had been in rigid religious orders for many lifetimes.

Ken broke his vows of past lifetimes, including several pledges to poverty and celibacy. We then informed him that he was in a recovery lifetime learning how to be in the world—which entailed earning money, having a family, and enjoying a creative life. Soon afterward, we had him call back the energies of those in his former religious orders to ask if his participation in the world would upset them. They explained that he was one of the last to move on and had in fact been holding back the evolution of the group. Relieved that he was not betraying his original commitment to God, he pledged his loyalty to his family and career.

The Significance of Body Reactions

Whenever an energy shift occurs, the body reacts. Jerks, twitching, skin color changes, breathing rate changes, tears, laughter, sighs, body or skin temperature changes, tingling, rolling of the eyes, and dilation of the pupils are all signs that energy is being released. The portion of the body in which a release occurs, its degree of prominence, and the triggering subject matter provide information about the nature and depth of the shift.

Energetic shifts occur in response to everything from a simple awareness to a major release of blocked energy. The deeper the shift is, the more pronounced the reaction will be.

MESSAGES FROM THE EMOTIONAL BODY

Many emotions are held in the emotional body without coming to direct expression in the physical body. Among those most deeply suppressed are sadness, anger, fear, frustration, jealousy, and pain. More often than not, these feelings can be accessed by paying close attention to subtle energetic cues.

While working with a client who is not shedding tears, for example, you may sense that her emotional body is crying. To confirm your hunch, check for redness in her face, or a sense of sadness or heaviness in the room. Then bring the situation to your client's attention by asking, "How do you feel?" or "What are you feeling?" or "Do you feel yourself crying?" In response, she will most likely allow herself to cry. Questions help reconnect people to their feelings.

CLUES TO THE DEEPER ISSUES

Healing surface-level symptoms will produce results in the sphere of personality, in which case the presenting symptoms may reappear. Clearing the *root cause*—the underlying emotional, mental, physical, or spiritual issue—will effect a profound and lasting change.

Working with an illness or other imbalance is much like pulling weeds. You can yank off its leaves, or even break its stem, yet the weed will survive. On the surface, there will be no sign of the culprit, yet the root system, still intact, will eventually produce new growth. Only when the *main* root is cleared away will the weed die.

So it is with healing. In fact, the sooner you identify the root cause of a problem, the quicker and more complete the healing will be. To reach beyond surface symptoms, ask yourself, "What is the underlying meaning here?" or ask your client, "What is the deeper issue?" or have her relax and reenter the situation or lifetime that gave rise to the trauma.

The Location of Symptoms

A person's physical pain, discomfort, or disease invariably expresses an unhealed issue from the present or a past lifetime. This is true of both a recurring pain that doctors cannot explain and a sudden, acute illness. In nearly all instances, the location of the problem can lead you to an understanding of how it was initiated.

Each part of the body is designed to perform a unique function and, in turn, bears the energetic imprint of traumas associated with it. The eyes, for instance, hold cues to sight and seeing; the mind, to thinking and memory; the hands and arms, to receiving, giving, or holding on; the hips to forward movement. (For additional information on these correspondences, please refer to Michael's book on healing energy.)

Once you know where a client's symptoms are located, simply quiet your mind and tune into her. Have her close her eyes and enter into a state of deep relaxation. When she is fully relaxed, ask her to search inwardly for a feeling, memory, picture, or word that awakens a sense of how and when the injury occurred. Remembering the original trauma, and then resolving it, will almost always eradicate the pain.

To assist in the recall, pose direct questions. If her throat is symptomatic, for example, ask, "What is stuck in your throat?" or "What are you afraid to say?" or "Who are you afraid of? What are you swallowing rather than speaking about?"

Alternatively, you can use the technique known as dialoguing, in which you state the beginning of a sentence and your client completes it. You might say, for example: "If my throat could talk, it would tell you _____." Then urge your client to continue filling in the blank until the answer feels complete to both of you. An emotional release usually breaks forth when the root cause is revealed.

Ellen, a beautician in her late forties, suffered from a recurring pain in her right arm and shoulder. Because the pain was on the right (masculine) side of her body and she clenched her right fist as she spoke, we concluded that she was dealing with suppressed anger. When we asked Ellen who she wanted to hit, she tapped into the anger and began screaming at her husband and calling him names. She told us she felt humiliated when her ex-husband betrayed her fourteen months before, and upset when she discovered he had stolen most of the money they had saved during their marriage. After a while, she cried and the pain subsided.

Jane, a minister in her mid-fifties, knew that something happened to her at age three but could recall no precipitating event. While speaking, she would move her hand to her throat and cough from time to time. We had the impression that she had been stabbed in the throat during a previous lifetime. When we asked her if this image meant anything to her, she remembered a lifetime in which she—a quiet, slight woman—confronted a man who seemed beyond reproach. Without warning, he pulled out a dagger and stabbed her in the throat.

We then asked her if this man was alive and in her life now. Immediately she said, "Oh, my God. It's my younger sister!" She proceeded to explain that when her sister was born she panicked and shut down her voice for fear of being killed again. At the time, she was three years old.

Body Fluids, Smells, and Sounds

Spirit intervenes in each moment of life. Signs of an emotional blockage that do not come forth in physical symptoms or words tend to emerge in the form of body fluids, smells, and sounds. Your task in such situations is to remain fearlessly alert to all dimensions, to follow all guidance, and to trust the process. Remember, you are not in charge—spirit is!

During several healing sessions, we noticed, oozing out of one or both of a client's eyes, a yellowish pus so thick the person could not see clearly. Accompanying each of these discharges was an emotional breakthrough associated with disease, injury, illness, blindness, or not wanting to see.

Claudia, a housewife in her mid-thirties, scheduled a private session because certain odors irritated her nose. We had her close her eyes and relax. When her breathing slowed down, we asked her if the problem originated in this lifetime. She said no. We asked her if it began in another lifetime, and she nodded yes. As we were working, we saw burning bodies and images of Germany in the 1940s. Something about the Holocaust, we assumed, lay at the root of her hypersensitivity.

Without sharing our vision, we asked Claudia to go back to the time she first experienced the irritation in her nose. She described ovens in great detail and the odor of burning bodies. The more she spoke, the more trauma she reexperienced, and the more the color drained from her face. We sensed her life force leaving her body and instinctively knew that unless we intervened quickly she might leave her body and die.

Michael decided to confront her. "You are now at a *choice point*," he said. "You can choose to either live and face this trauma now or die and face it in another lifetime." Rosalie reminded her, "One way or another, you are going to have to resolve this trauma." We prayed and held loving energy for Claudia while she made her decision. She elected to face the pain, whereupon the color slowly returned to her face and we successfully completed the session.

Flora, a dietitian in her late thirties, attended a workshop we were conducting. As she closed her eyes and turned inward, the room filled with the odor of burning wood. At first we thought something in the house was on fire. Then we asked her if she had ever been burned alive. She screamed and burst into tears, at which point the fervor of her emotions matched the intensity of the smell. As her trauma subsided, so did the odor, until it vanished completely. She later told the group that she remembered being burned alive because she had refused to identify other members of a secret group of spiritual seekers.

We left the workshop with an indelible reminder that all the sensory accompaniments of trauma become trapped in the human energy field. We had no doubt that Flora's soul, in releasing the scent of burning wood, had guided us to the healing she needed.

Jane, a professional athlete in her early forties, had been raped in this lifetime and, she suspected, in previous ones as well. While we energetically cleared her energy field, using the sexual abuse clearing technique outlined in chapter 12, the room filled with the strong odor of sperm. (*Note:* The odor of sperm has been evident in a number of sessions involving rape or childhood sexual abuse in the present or a past lifetime. Sometimes the odor is released through the person's mouth; other times, it shows up as a general suffusion in the room.)

Susan, a retired executive in her late fifties, had reached an impasse in a workshop. No matter what we did, we could not assist her in breaking through. We stopped, quieted ourselves, and asked for spiritual guidance. Right away, we were given the image of a pair of hands playing a flute. Confused about the meaning of the flute, we asked for assistance and received the same picture. After our third request, and third appearance of the image, Michael asked her, "What does someone playing a flute mean to you?"

Within seconds, strains of flute music had become audible to nearly everyone in the room, including Susan, who suddenly appeared calmer. To this day, we do not know what the flute meant to her or why she needed to hear it. Spirit, it seems, is smarter than we are and knows just what is needed for a healing.

Part 3
SOUL-BASED HEALING

THE DYNAMICS OF HEALING

* *

"Spirit and body alike require honesty and integrity to thrive.
For that reason we inherently need to rid ourselves of
all distortions that we have created."

—Caroline Myss

W E WERE ALL RAISED in families that were at least moderately dysfunctional. To make sense of our world, we shut down our feelings, internalized limiting belief systems, and developed personality strategies such as resistance, projection, or denial. Our bodies adapted and adjusted until, no longer able to compensate, they succumbed to illness of one sort or another.

Lodged deep within our minds are memories of the painful experiences that initially caused us to alter our approach to life. In fact, stored within the chambers of this great repository is a complete rendering of our current lifetime, past lifetimes, and soul essence. To locate the revealing pieces of information, weed out the destructive patterns, and realign with our essence nature, we first need to learn how the mind functions.

THE MIND: AN INSTRUMENT OF HEALING

The mind is an interactive network composed of the conscious mind, the subconscious mind, and the superconscious mind. The *conscious mind* is the gatekeeper, whose job it is to vigilantly compare, judge, and edit the information that comes our way. Prompted by the attitudes and belief systems it has internalized, it assigns a positive or negative emotional value to each of our ongoing experiences. If these attitudes and beliefs are congruent with our soul essence, the conscious mind can be our best friend, spurring us on to states of harmony and balance. If it has been programmed with false data, it can be our worst enemy, walling us off from our emotions and even rejecting information crucial to our well-being.

The *subconscious mind* houses a detailed historical record of our sojourns on the earth plane, including a full-color moving picture complete with sounds, smells, tastes, and tactile sensations. The only time this information surfaces to awareness is when it is activated by the conscious mind. The subconscious mind does not employ reason; nor does it place a value judgment or an emotional charge on experiences. It merely responds to suggestions.

The *superconscious mind* links us to our essence and the wisdom of the universe. It is accessed directly through intuition, prayer, meditation, or focused intention. Often a phrase, such as "Knock and the door shall open" or "Ask and ye shall receive," will usher us across the threshold. Here we find that whatever we focus our attention on we attract. The superconcious mind, which is pure thought, can instantly manifest information and miraculous healings.

Every technique described in this book utilizes all three parts of the mind to promote healing. They encourage the conscious mind to open the gate to subconscious memories and also activate the superconscious mind to illuminate our soul purpose. Healing stimulated in this way takes place simultaneously on the emotional, mental, physical, and spiritual levels.

ACCESSING YOUR FEELINGS

The primary cause of out-of-balance states such as distress, frustration, pain, and physical illness is a blockage of emotional energy most often introduced and reinforced by a dysfunctional family system. Just as adult members of dysfunctional families have been trained to neglect, judge, and override their needs and feelings in favor of taking care of others, so have their children. To survive, they learn early on to invalidate, ignore, and suppress their authentic emotions. They also learn to distrust nonfamily members, which further separates them from healthy role models who feel their feelings and excel in clear styles of communication. Many adult children from dysfunctional families have majored in "looking good" and enabling others to look good, too.

Locked away beneath the facade sustained by the conscious mind is a full-sensory moving picture of all that has occurred, including the damming up of one emotion after another, along with the attendant pain and remorse. What appears on the surface, though, is flawless, other than an occasional eruption of honesty. Following are three of the most telling signs that something is askew.

Limiting Belief Systems

A limiting belief is a programmed tenet that undermines our multidimensional nature. Whereas some limiting beliefs reside in the conscious mind, others are concealed in the subconscious mind.

Peggy, a teacher in her late forties, had a difficult childhood. Her alcoholic father was physically abusive to the family, and her mother was not strong enough to take care of herself or the children. As a teenager, Peggy assumed the role of adult and arranged for her mother and two younger sisters to move to another town, relocating along with them. In adulthood she supported her mother and provided her sisters with a college education. Romantic relationships, however, did not come easily. When she started falling in love with one man, she told him, "I'm afraid that if I open my heart to you I will never be able to take care of myself again!" The relationship ended. To this day Peggy remains single.

Self-Fulfilling Prophecies

A self-fulfilling prophecy is a fear-based prediction that comes true because we energetically attract the dreaded outcome. Fear, which keeps us trapped in negative expectations, can engender a series of self-fulfilling prophecies. In many ways it is like a living organism that feeds off of ongoing experiences. Beneath the fear is long-buried pain.

For many people, the need to be right is so great that they will validate their fears by destroying what they most desire. Those who are afraid of love will create the illusion that they are not receiving love, even when they are. Those who are afraid of being supported will blow holes in their support systems. Those who fear they will never succeed will sabotage themselves on the road to success.

Self-fulfilling prophecies adhere to the second universal law. The first, the law of karma, states that "what we do to others comes back to us"; the second, the divine law, maintains that "what we do to ourselves comes back to us." When we fail to honor, nurture, or care for ourselves, we attract people and situations that give us the experience of being unacknowledged. When we are bitter, angry, and resentful toward ourselves, we attract people who appear to be bitter, angry, and resentful toward us.

Bill and Sarah, a couple in their late forties, carried unresolved pains from childhood and from previously broken marriages. Bill, rejected by his father, had never been accepted by his family of origin. He was convinced he was not good enough. Sarah had taken most of the blame in her family. She was certain that she could do nothing right and that she attracted only men who took advantage of her financially.

Bill loved Sarah and longed to buy her presents. One day he confessed that he wanted to buy her a house with a white picket fence. "I'm not for sale," she replied. "You can't buy me!" Bill, having opened his heart and decided at long last to settle down, felt rejected once again. And Sarah, who had often complained about not being supported by men, placed herself in yet another unsupportable position. Their self-fulfilling prophecies had interlocked, resulting in double ruination.

Double Binds

A double bind is an either-or predicament in which both choices keep us out of alignment with our soul purpose and soul agreements. Rather than respond to the situation authentically, we become immobilized by our limiting beliefs and react automatically. Signs of a double bind include feelings of low self-esteem and an incapacity to have a positive impact, lack of motivation, and a sense of helplessness, frustration, limited satisfaction, and hopelessness.

Nina, an architect in her early forties, wanted to become a healer. At the same time, she was terrified of becoming accomplished in this arena. She ended up withdrawing from every healing arts program in which she enrolled.

Susan, a business manager in her early thirties, suffered from low self-esteem. Although she wanted to join a country club, she was certain any country club that would have her wasn't "worth joining." Regardless of the establishments she visited, she remained trapped in her lose-lose perspective.

Opening to Feelings

If you have perfected any of these communication patterns, you can reasonably assume that you are harboring painful emotions. To heal, you will need to acknowledge, even welcome, all your feelings—a feat that will take practice and perseverance. Success is guaranteed, provided that you encourage your conscious mind to release the personality defenses it has forged and align with your soul purpose.

At first, you may decide that the recovery of feelings is not worth your time and effort, or that you would prefer to bypass your pain and grief. After contacting some of your feelings, you may say, with exasperation, "I can't get it right" or "What's the use?" In such moments, please remember that abandoning the process will only further distance you from your essence. For support, turn instead to prayer, meditation, affirmations, and journaling.

The simplest way to access your feelings is to catch yourself overreacting. Any time you begin attacking, withdrawing, blaming, or complaining, stop, take a few deep breaths, and step back from the encounter. In other words, become the observer. From this vantage point, attempt to see the value in replacing your ineffective communication patterns with clear requests. Instead of blaming and complaining, learn to ask for what you need.

Here is one good way to begin. While continuing to feel your emotions, spend 5 minutes or more reflecting on each of the following questions. Write out your answers, if you wish.

How do I feel?

Naming your emotions will remind you to be honest with yourself.

How intense are these feelings?

If your reaction is relatively mild, you are most likely grappling with a current lifetime issue. If you are out of control, the situation may have triggered an unresolved past-life trauma. The intensity, duration, and frequency of your reaction will let you know the extent of the suppressed trauma. Whether the incident transpired in this lifetime or a previous one, this exercise will prove effective.

Where in my body do I experience the sensations?

Relax and trace your feelings to specific places in your body. Notice how your body reacts. Locating the seat of pent-up emotions is sometimes enough to guide you to old wounds, at which point you can release the energy locked within them.

When in my past did I experience similar emotions?

Recall earlier incidents, including the people you were with. As you focus your intention on past circumstances, your mind will begin scanning for earlier evidence of overreactions. In response you may experience a sudden flash of awareness.

What is my earliest memory of these feelings?

Identifying the root cause of your emotional response will help you examine past decisions associated with it, assess the degree to which they currently serve you, and, if necessary, release them.

If you cannot remember what happened, ask your subconscious mind for a dream revealing the initial trauma and your subsequent decisions.

Forgive and release the past! Healing unresolved issues from times gone by will often clear the emotional charge emitted in present situations. At the very least, it will free you to honestly express your feelings and needs. Before reengaging in the stormy encounter, decide on how best to take care of yourself. Is the present interaction serving you? Can you negotiate a truce? Would it be better to continue communicating or to stop the exchange?

IDENTIFYING DYSFUNCTIONAL FAMILY PATTERNS

Among the patterns most damaging to healthy development are the subtle, unspoken messages devaluing a child's self-worth and multidimensionality. These violations can leave deep emotional scars, obstructing the child's energy flow and keeping him cut off from his essence nature. Only by eventually identifying the insidious dynamic, stored deep within his subconscious mind, will he be able to release the experience of abuse and accelerate the evolution of his soul.

Emotional Incest

Emotional incest—a phenomenon more prevalent than sexual incest, though less discussed—supervenes when fathers, mothers, stepparents, or other relatives bond inappropriately with a child to fill an emotional void in their lives. In such situations the child is no longer respected as a youngster with wants, needs, and desires of his own.

This form of incest is difficult to identify because on the surface it often appears as an act of caring and loving. A father, for example, may call his daughter "Daddy's little girl," and may attempt to emotionally seduce her by asking, "When you grow up, can I marry you?" A divorced mother may tell her young son, "You are now the man of the house." In two-parent households, victims of emotional incest become caught, like an extramarital lover, between mom and dad. Those in single-parent households end up attempting to take care of the parent. Always, codependency and self-sacrifice rule the roost.

As emotionally incested children mature, they begin to doubt their ability to flourish emotionally beyond the parameters of the parent bond. Most are unable to relate appropriately to other adults. Many have difficulty bonding with a mate and creating a family of their own. Some remain at home most of their lives, relying on the parent for their sense of self-esteem.

Paula, a divorced woman in her thirties, had a nine-year-old son. At the age of six, he would crawl into bed with her whenever he was scared. Because she liked having someone to curl up with, they spent the next three years sleeping in each other's arms at night. They also spent endless hours together during the day. Paula was proud of their closeness and told people they were best friends.

With so little free time, this mother seldom dated and had only a handful of adult friends. On a few occasions she brought a man home to meet her son, but the child invariably threw a temper tantrum and started fights, enraged that she was not spending her time with him. He was eventually removed from public school because he refused to do his homework, lied to his teacher, and was both verbally and physically abusive. By age nine, he was uncontrollable.

Harry and Barbara were married in their mid-thirties. At the time, Harry was looking for security and Barbara wanted children. Although she knew Harry did not want a family, she tricked him into conceiving. Soon afterward, she gave birth to a son and made him the center of her life. Each time Harry explained that he, too, needed attention, she accused him of being selfish. Feeling left out, resentful, and extremely angry, he blamed his son for the loss of his wife.

Five years later Barbara gave birth to a daughter. At last, Harry found that he had someone to love. As she grew older, he spent more and more time with her, eventually confiding in her about his unhappy marriage. She, in turn, learned to take care of her father's needs and serve as a peer. Both children, now in their forties, are divorced and unable to sustain long-term relationships.

Although the family bonds that underlie emotional incest may feel loving, the child's loss of boundaries poses identity problems. If this form of abuse rings true to you, prepare for a distressing yet liberating quest. It takes tremendous courage to confront one's family system, reevaluate the dynamics prevalent in childhood, and examine whether one was truly loved or manipulated into fulfilling a parent's needs. The truth can be heartbreaking. Admitting to yourself that you were used, however, can spur you on to healthier ways of interacting and provide an opportunity for healing.

Wounds to the Inner Child

Early in life, the inner child is a wellspring of joy, spontaneity, and creativity, desiring only unconditional love. By the age of five or six, the inner child has often become unhappy, angry, manipulative, frightened, or lost—in short, wounded. Unprotected by psychic boundaries, it has absorbed both the spoken and unspoken emotions of the family.

In some instances, the wounded inner child carries the expressed and unexpressed rage of the parents. In others, it holds a profusion of parental judgments. Rarely, however, is this content addressed. The conspiracy of silence that governs most dysfunctional families repeatedly discounts the tumultuous inner world of the child. Denial sets in, and becomes reinforced each time the child acknowledges that something has indeed happened but is no longer able to feel it.

Tricia, a thirty-two-year-old postal worker, remembered being joyful, imaginative, and spontaneous as a young child. She dreamed of becoming an actress. At age six, her parents shamed her because of her trust and openness. After that, she silenced herself, retreating further and further inward until she had nearly isolated herself from life.

Ralph, a forty-eight-year-old accountant, was lethargic and unassertive. When he was a child, he said, his parents ignored him, called him names, and refused to support or encourage him in his interests. "Family is all you need," they told him. As a youngster, he feared social situations, and by his twenties he had become an introvert.

Sensitive to the wounds of the inner child, psychologist Virginia Satir would ask her clients, "Is your past illuminating your present or contaminating it?" If you are harboring a wounded inner child and would like to move toward illumination, begin by granting the child amnesty. Recover it in all its woundedness, and grieve the years of lost innocence.

As your subconscious mind reveals forgotten memories, you may feel angry upon discovering that a sacred part of you was not acknowledged. Be sure to address this anger, no matter how much vulnerability it arouses. Express your rage, give voice to blame, then articulate the desires or expectations that were never recognized. Finally, urge your inner child to practice communicating with nonthreatening people, by saying, "I want you to hear what I am feeling" and "What I would like is _____ ." Speaking the truth is a healing essential!

Having liberated your wounded inner child, *you* will be the one to appreciate and nurture its spontaneity, creativity, and delight. You will also be in a position to offer forgiveness—to your parents as well as yourself.

Shame

Shame, a gnawing sense of humiliation and disgrace, originates as an overlay of a dysfunctional family system designed to keep its members locked in suffering and alienation. Shame attacks are targeted against children because of their gender, enthusiasm, emotional sensitivity, physical assets, sexuality, learning styles, or expressions of individuality. Victims of these attacks experience feelings ranging from self-contempt to overwhelming despair. Whereas guilt—an overlay of its own—is about doing or not doing, shame is about *being*.

Shame carries a dense vibration that feels like a heavy weight. Self-esteem turns to self-doubt and confusion. Victims of shame attacks, believing they are unworthy of being in relationship, seek safety in invisibility and inaudibility. In uncomfortable situations, they will regress to the age at which the shaming began, rendering them even more powerless. Unacknowledged shame is often experienced as spiritual bitterness.

Sophia, a forty-nine-year-old dental assistant, had been resentful and depressed most of her life. When she was born, her parents were disappointed that she was not a boy. They rarely paid attention to her as a child, and when they did, they belittled her. Despite her ongoing attempts to please them, she never felt loved or accepted. When she came for a session, she was bitter toward everyone, and God as well.

If these symptoms sound familiar to you, remember that consciousness expands to encompass everything you concentrate on and affirm. To mentally activate your healing, focus on your inherent worthiness. Remind yourself that you are entitled to be in a healthy relationship and to actively participate in your own evolution. In one sense, recovery from shame rebuilds self-esteem, the foundation for personal empowerment. In another, the movement from disgrace to grace can be the journey of a lifetime!

INTEGRATING PAST LIFETIMES

The soul lives through hundreds, if not thousands, of incarnations. Past-life experiences that are not integrated into the present often exert such a powerful influence that they interfere with our ability to make important decisions. Under the influence of bleedthrough from the past, we fail to act like ourselves. We lapse into automatic behavior, as if we have slipped into a psychic black hole. Past-life recall—which can range from partial to total—often requires the assistance of a healer familiar with the soul's operating principles.

An unresolved past-life trauma will go to any extreme to attract our attention. Some people will face a crisis triggered by a similar event in this lifetime. Others, upon approaching the age at which they were previously traumatized, will begin trekking through an emotional minefield, suddenly exhibiting the same behaviors as before. Unintegrated lifetimes show up as irrational thoughts, volatile emotions, or disruptive actions. They also cause a variety of physical or emotional illnesses, such as chronic fatigue syndrome (ME) and multiple personality disorder.

To integrate a bleedthrough lifetime on your own, ask yourself, "Where and in what lifetime did this experience actually originate?"

Or ask: "What is the true cause of this situation? What is the magnet lifetime? What do I need in order to integrate it into the present?" All the while use prayer, intuition, and focused intention to elicit assistance from your superconcious mind.

Helen and Ralph, a couple in their late forties, had reached an impasse in their marriage. Helen was inconsolable after the death of her dog, which had been her animal ally for fifteen years. Ralph commented: "In all my life I have never seen anyone grieve like this. Nothing I do seems to matter. Contact is impossible. Life has lost all meaning to her." Helen, we discovered, had entered a past lifetime bleedthrough.

We asked this couple if they would be willing to explore a past lifetime they both remembered. They agreed, whereupon we reminded them that our goal was to extract their souls' organizing principles so we could gain perspective on their predicament. Helen began by reconnecting with a lifetime in which she was the proud and adoring mother of her present partner. She described herself as a young woman whose position in the community had been enhanced by his birth. The entire village rejoiced.

Ralph nodded and said that he could recall enjoying the adoration of his mother and the welcome prepared by the villagers. But his memories of that lifetime, he explained, seemed to fade out when he was about three years old.

Helen went on to recall that at age seven, her son was ripped away from her to be groomed for leadership by his father, who by then had remarried. Ralph cried as he remembered his daddy's friends ordering him to be quiet because if he screamed and woke up his mother, they would kill her. Frightened, he did as he was told.

Helen never learned what happened to her son. All she knew from that point on was grief, which shrouded her life and robbed her of all happiness.

In the present lifetime, as in the prior one, Ralph did not know what to do. Words were useless; contact, impossible. Both individuals felt disconnected from each other, detached from their world, and hopeless. Recognizing that they could now move beyond the organizing principles of grief and abandonment, we invited Ralph to fight for the relationship, as he was now a man with power. At the same time, we encouraged Helen to experience her grief and to trust that Ralph would support her.

He hugged her and she rested in his arms, crying. "All I need to know is that you are here," she told him.

"I want to give you more than that," he replied.

For this couple, isolating the magnet lifetime was similar to piercing an abscess. Helen continued to grieve for her dog, but now her conscious mind knew that healing was possible.

Paulette, a fifteen year old with chronic fatigue syndrome (ME) had been too physically depleted to attend school for three years. We discovered that as a young teenager in a previous lifetime, she had been away from home when her mother committed suicide. Haunted by guilt, she was certain that had she remained at home, her mother would have lived. Upon entering adolescence in this lifetime Paulette, obsessed with fear that her mother would die, sacrificed her friendships, three years of education, and her well-being to guarantee her mother's safety.

We began by helping Paulette release the bleedthrough trauma of her former mother's death. We then insisted that she tell her present mother the truth; and we encouraged her mother, in turn, to offer reassurances that she was not going to die. Soon afterward, we were able to clear the illness, whereupon Paulette returned to school knowing that her mother would survive her absence.

Carmen, a health club owner in her late thirties, had a history of painful menstrual cramps. Her husband jokingly called her a "Tasmanian devil" because of the intensity of anger that accompanied her menstruation. While working with Carmen, we asked her if the cause of her pain was from this lifetime or another. She indicated that it was from a previous life. Upon reentering the magnet lifetime, she saw herself among a group of girls in a temple. "We were virgins who were going to be sacrificed at the time of our first menstrual cycles," she explained.

We asked her how she felt about being sacrificed. She said she was scared and angry. A moment later she screamed, then reported an immediate release in her abdomen. The entire session lasted less than twenty minutes. In a follow-up discussion a few months later, both she and her husband confirmed that the healing was complete.

Carmen's case is not unique. In our experience, most women who have problems at the time of their menstrual cycles find a link with either past-life memories or early adolescent prohibitions against the display of anger at any time other than menstruation.

Harriet, by her late thirties, had traveled around the world commanding great respect for her spiritual gifts. Despite the many people she had helped, she was averse to being touched by anyone other than close friends. Not even her physician was permitted to touch her.

When we met with Harriet, we felt we had to work quickly or she would dash off. After an opening prayer, we invited her to free the fears that were separating her from a physical connection with others. She soon saw a past lifetime in which she was burned alive at the stake, surrounded by throngs of people. Although fire encircled her, she reported, the flames never touched her. Finally, the people took her down from the stake and tried to kill her, yet she somehow survived. At that point, she burst into tears and allowed us to hold her.

Days later, she phoned to say she had no problem being touched. She experienced no follow-up trauma, and was able to proceed with her life.

All these sessions brought about profound transformation. In each instance, we began by accessing the individual's essence through the superconscious mind. Working with the person's conscious mind, we then gained entry into the subconscious mind to access memories causing the blockage of emotional energy. After identifying the trauma, we appealed to the person's conscious mind to resolve the turmoil and allow for healing.

Eight

What to Expect from a Healing Session

* * * * * * * * * * * * * * *

"Transformation marks the end of an accidental life and the beginning of a deliberate life that is lived from the inside out."

—Kathleen Noble

THE OBJECTIVE of a healing session is to increase a person's connection to his essence self, which leads to enhanced spontaneity, extended emotional availability, and freedom from guilt, shame, and judgment. The energetic outcome is a greater energy flow on all levels of one's being. Benefits usually include improved relationships, an increased likelihood of success and prosperity, a more positive outlook on life, improved health, and a deepened spiritual connection.

If you wish to augment your self-healing endeavors in these arenas, a healing session is highly recommended. It can help you further clarify your life direction, while releasing the trauma and blocked energy of this and other lifetimes.

But prepare for some initial resistance. Before scheduling your appointment, you may have second thoughts sparked by old patterns of protection, ingrained defenses, or pretenses that have sustained you all these years. Rest assured, old habits can be transformed, and your guides and teachers will support you in aligning with your essence.

Preparing for a Healing Session

Preparation is essential. Before your appointment, reflect upon what you hope to gain from the session, the questions you wish to ask, and the patterns you would like to heal. You may even want to commit these goals to paper. In clarifying your objectives, be sure to ask your guides for help. It is your responsibility to ask for guidance, and theirs to assist you in fulfilling your soul purpose.

Time and Health Concerns

Avoid all addictive substances for at least twenty-four hours prior to the session, as well as forty-eight hours afterward. On the day of your appointment, arrange for an hour of relaxation before meeting with the healer, about an hour for the session, and an hour or two of uninterrupted integration time afterward. Plan ahead so you will arrive relatively relaxed and willing to be as open as possible, positive, and focused on your commitment to healing.

Fears and Doubts

Prior to a healing session, the personality often becomes uneasy or scared, because it recognizes that change is imminent. Reluctant to forfeit control over the person's life, it sends out ripples of fear, doubt, and insecurity which, if not addressed, will indeed interfere with healing.

If you experience any of the personality dynamics listed below, understand that this reaction is normal. Breathe through your resistance and reaffirm your choice to align with your essence. (*Note:* These hindrances may also show up during or even after your session. If they do, recognize them one by one as a limiting belief and reaffirm your decision to say yes to your soul purpose.)

◆ Fear of change, losing control, the unknown
◆ Fear of feeling your feelings
◆ Fear of committing to your healing

- Fear of making decisions that may upset people
- Fear of power
- Fear of being in your body and fully experiencing life
- Fear of being "trapped" on the earth plane
- Fear of love, joy, and happiness
- Fear of making a wrong decision
- Fear of spiritual gifts and experiences
- Fear of going crazy
- Fear of finding out that you are not perfect
- Fear of releasing past-life vows, promises and commitments
- Denial that a problem exists
- Lack of faith in yourself or the healer
- Lack of discernment in your devotion to parents, culture, country, or religion
- Failure to believe in a higher power
- Belief that past events are unimportant
- Belief that you don't have a right to be more joyful (successful, creative, conscious) than your parents
- Belief in the need for struggle, pain, and suffering

Excuses for Giving Up

Over many years of assisting people in realigning with their essence nature, we have listened to hundreds of learned limitations that contribute to a sense of low self-esteem, powerlessness, mediocrity, and codependence. These half-truths—all stated as "reasons" for forgoing a healing session—are, like fears and doubts, promptings from a personality unwilling to surrender its control.

Below is a list of some of the most frequently cited promptings. If you catch yourself verbalizing one or more of these statements, realize that you are at a choice point: It is time to say yes to either the dictates of your personality or the evolution of your soul.

- "It will never work anyway."
- "I don't have the energy."
- "I can't do it alone."
- "I have to do it by myself."

- "It's not the right time."
- "I'm too scared."
- "What if I don't like myself after I change?"
- "I'm too ashamed."
- "I'm incapable of forgiving myself or others."
- "If I heal, I will have to take responsibility for my life."
- "I'm afraid that if I feel my anger I'll kill someone."
- "It's the way I was brought up; it's all I know."
- "No matter what you or I do, it will never fill the hole within me."
- "I'm afraid of losing control."
- "I'm afraid of being judged."
- "I can't afford it."
- "Why bother? My parents didn't want me, so how could anyone else?"

THE HEALING SESSION

Do your best to arrive in a state of unconditional love and unconditional thinking that will allow you to regard yourself with an expanded consciousness of possibilities. Prepare to inform the healer of the reason for your visit and the nature of your goals. Plan on having your unconditional loving and thinking fully supported. Count on receiving information from your subconscious and superconscious minds that will reacquaint you with your spiritual context.

Most of all, expect to be surprised. Even if you arrive with a clear idea of what is needed for your healing, energy will follow need, and there is no way to anticipate just what that may be. Promises made to yourself or others may come up for review. Soul agreements formed with people you know may announce themselves, adding clarity to your relationships. Inspirited ones—either unborn children or deceased friends or family members—may communicate with you. You may gain insight into the deeper meaning of an ailment or illness, or discover a link between a physical condition and resistance to your essence. One thing is certain: You will experience the dance between your conscious, subconscious, and superconscious minds as they cocreate the next stage in your evolution.

FOLLOW-UP CARE

Before leaving the session, drink a large glass of water to help ground you. Continue to drink plenty of water over the next forty-eight hours to flush out the toxins released during the session. Toxins that are not discharged from the body will be reabsorbed.

Immediate Concerns

The time spent immediately after a healing session is as significant as the time spent in the session. This quiet interlude of an hour or two is for integrating the healing energies and reflecting on what you learned. Allow yourself to simply be with the experience, rather than try to figure it out. Perhaps visit a favorite place of relaxation, walk in nature, or write. Whatever activity you decide on, steer clear of drugs, alcohol, negative people, crowds, noise, and stressful situations. Do not return to work for at least two hours.

To cleanse the auric field around the body, we recommend a hot bath in the evening. Bathwater mixed with one cup of either apple cider vinegar, Epsom salts, or sea salt will help stimulate the release of toxins through the skin. Remember to slip your head underwater, too.

Common Aftereffects

The release of blocked energy will lead to either an increase or decrease in vitality, as well as a wide range of emotions. This energetic shift is a sign that your body's meridians have opened for healing. To smooth the way to recovery, be willing to feel all your emotions without judgment or attachment.

Many women begin menstruating within hours of a healing session. Most often, the trigger for this phenomenon is the release of long-suppressed energy associated with trauma. Sometimes it is the release of fear about being a woman.

Positive Feelings—Most people feel lively, self-confident, clear, joyful, happy, peaceful, and free. They also feel more connected to their bodies and their inner sources of guidance. Clients often speak of feeling their hearts "open" or of having a "honeymoon" with themselves. This euphoria can last for hours or for the rest of your life. The high, however, is not the goal; soul empowerment is. Realigned with your soul essence, you will both internalize and radiate optimism, abundance, harmony, a sense of inner knowing, and joy.

Headaches—Causes for throbbing temples include:

- Struggling to figure out or control the post-session experience
- Feeling guilty about an incident faced in the session and judged
- Resistance to change
- Fear of authenticity
- Discharge of old, inappropriate programming
- Release of toxins from the brain
- Opening spiritually. Pain in the third eye and crown chakra area, in particular, can be triggered by the memory of past-life trauma.

At the onset of a headache, breathe into the pain. Love yourself unconditionally. Drink lots of water and take a hot bath to cleanse the auric field, as described above. Then rest and surrender even more deeply to the healing.

Flu-like Symptoms—Fever is an indication that the body is burning up old memory patterns. Body aches and pains are the result of tension. At the first sign of discomfort, acknowledge your feelings and express them through art, dance, poetry, or conversations with a friend.

Fatigue—Exhaustion is precipitated by tension, resistance, or the depletion of energy used for healing. If you feel tired, allow yourself to slow down and rest. The integration time needed after a healing session is comparable to the recovery time required after surgery.

Anger—Most often, the anger that surfaces is old, suppressed indignation that could not be safely expressed to parents or other authority figures. Sometimes it is rage directed at oneself for a failure to meet personal expectations or the demands of others. In either instance, the feelings are coming up for release. Healing will follow as long as the anger is not judged.

If anger or rage erupts, feel free to scream or hit a soft object, such as a pillow. Whatever you do, *avoid directing your anger at a person, animal, or solid object.* Strenuous physical exercise is also effective. All the while, ask yourself, "Who am I really angry at? What happened to me? When did it happen?" Tell your conscious mind that you are ready to know the truth, then invite the memories to come up for healing. Or dialogue with yourself and write about your thoughts and feelings.

Fear—Fear tends to arise in the form of questions, such as "Who will understand me?" "Who will love me?" "How should I act?" If you become engulfed by fear, breathe into it, filling yourself with white light and unconditional love. Remember that you are a multi-dimensional being, and call upon the support of your soul affiliations as well as divine love. Each fear that you face in this way will lose its grip on you.

Loneliness—Releasing a loved one, an outgrown pattern, an addiction, or even a psychic cord can give way to feelings of sadness, loss, and grief. Terminating a dysfunctional relationship or saying good-bye to old friends can prompt similar emotions. When beset by loss, allow yourself to grieve, all the while filling yourself with white light and unconditional love. If a completion ceremony is in order, try lighting a candle, saying a prayer, or burning or burying an object related to the person or the habit.

Shaking—Body tremors are usually induced by a reluctance to release dysfunctional patterns and move on in life. Severe instances of shaking are often associated with a past-life trauma and a fear that opening up will lead to annihilation. If you suddenly begin shaking, ask yourself, "Am I releasing energy or am I holding back energy?" If you are obstructing the passage of energy, ask inwardly, "Why am I afraid of letting go?" Then unconditionally love yourself, drink lots of water, take a hot bath as described above, surrender to the shaking, and affirm that you are healing. If the shaking persists, consult with your healer.

A Healing Crisis—A major breakthrough or significant energy release is sometimes followed by a healing crisis marked by a combination of the symptoms described above, together with confusion, disorientation, and frustration. Cleared of outmoded patterns or negative attitudes and belief systems, the individual is in uncharted territory with no familiar landmarks. This situation resolves with the gradual discovery of new ways of being.

If you feel a healing crisis coming on, trust that although you have relinquished your old crutches you will survive without them. Remember, energy seeks balance. Your healing may have triggered deeper levels of suppressed energy, which often takes twenty-four to forty-eight hours to rebalance. In the meantime rest, drink lots of water, and pamper yourself. If you need support, call your healer.

ACTIVITIES TO AVOID OVER THE NEXT FORTY-EIGHT HOURS

To stabilize and bond with your cleared energy field, abstain from the following behaviors and activities:

◆ Engaging in sexual intercourse
◆ Making major decisions about relationship or career changes. This is not the time to fall in love, separate, commit to a marriage or divorce, or alter your work situation.
◆ Explaining the breakthrough to people who will not understand it
◆ Processing the experience with friends and family before fully integrating it yourself
◆ Intellectualizing the experience
◆ Venting your anger at anyone
◆ Blaming someone else for your pain
◆ Becoming too preoccupied to integrate the experience
◆ Being hard on yourself
◆ Thinking that change cannot be this easy
◆ Giving up on the learning available to you
◆ Believing that the healer is responsible for the healing
◆ Closing your eyes to the beauty and divinity within you

Supporting the Healing Process in the Days to Come

Healing is not a one-time fix. To the contrary, it requires ongoing reinforcement and a willingness to take complete responsibility for yourself. As you return to your day-to-day realities, build in several of the following activities to sustain your healing process:

- Rest, eat healthy foods, breathe clean air, drink plenty of water.
- Exercise—practice yoga, tai chi, stretching.
- Enjoy nature—hike in the woods, swim in a natural body of water.
- Spend time with supportive friends and groups.
- Set boundaries appropriate to your time and energy levels.
- Laugh and be playful.
- Listen to your inner guidance; communicate with your inner child.
- Exercise your capacity to be in your power and in your love.
- Create a safe, sacred environment for yourself.
- Be gentle with yourself; honor the timing of your process.
- Meditate and maintain a positive outlook.
- Indulge in a massage or other forms of bodywork.
- Do anger release work.
- Use flower essences to support the renewed harmony of your energetic field.
- Use affirmations and prayers to reinforce positive qualities.
- Reflect on moments of excellence.
- Feel your feelings without judging them.
- Practice taking risks and telling the truth.
- Keep a journal of positive changes.
- Cleanse your energy field by smudging with sage.
- Focus on positive energy by burning a white candle.

- Concentrate on your goals and your heart's desire.
- Listen to soft music; buy yourself flowers.
- Make a dream list.

How to Know If You Need Another Healing Session

If you feel stuck, scared, disoriented, or depressed, a follow-up session is recommended. A second session is also advised if you slip into a rage or if additional issues arise that you cannot work through on your own.

Nine

GUIDELINES FOR CONDUCTING
A HEALING SESSION

* * * * * * * * * * * * * * * * * *

"The world is a conscious field in which you and I are particles."

—Joseph Campbell

I N HEALING SESSIONS you will be presented with the illusion that your clients are confused, ill, or stricken with a terminal illness. Remember that this image is deceptive and that the greatest gift you can give your clients is to see beyond their challenges, behold their perfection, and regard them as multidimensional beings capable of creating miracles while aligned with the bylaws of their being. The guidelines that follow will help you sustain this perspective and keep yourself aligned as well.

PREPARING FOR A HEALING SESSION

Preparation is as critical to you as it is to your client. In many instances your readiness to be of service will depend not so much on the steps you take immediately prior to the session but rather on how you conduct your day-to-day life.

Ground Yourself

It is essential to stay grounded on the earth plane while accessing other dimensions. As someone once told us, "Spiritual work is like the old-fashioned trolley cars: You need to stay connected to the power lines above while keeping your wheels on the tracks. If either connection is broken, you go nowhere!" The more grounded you are, the easier it will be to connect with spiritual energies.

Try this grounding technique. Imagine a ball of intense white light coming down from the "source," and imagine the top of your head opening up to receive this pure energy. As the ball of light enters through the top of your head and moves down your spine, envision it cleansing, healing, and blessing each of your chakras, or energy centers. Allow the ball of energy to pass out of your base chakra and into the earth, until it reaches the center of the planet. Pause for a moment and feel your connection to the center of the earth. Then, leaving some of this energy there, bring the ball back up through the earth and your body, until it reaches your heart center. Fill your heart center with this special energy. When your heart is overflowing, send the energy out to your client through your heart, eyes, and hands.

Here is another technique to try. Imagine that you are a giant tree, perhaps a California redwood, with roots extending deep into the earth. Now activate as many of your senses as possible. See, hear, taste, and smell the earth; feel the soil in its interior. Once you are grounded, move your senses to the top of the tree, the sky above, and all that exists beyond the sky. Radiate this grounded expansiveness to your client.

In addition, you can ground yourself by becoming a beacon for your soul affiliations. As you link up with them, you will feel more at home, and you will soon be overflowing with blessings. (To increase your familiarity with your soul affiliations, see the meditation on page 193.)

On a daily basis as well, do whatever you can to stay grounded in your body. Eat root vegetables, take cold showers, drink lots of water, practice yoga, exercise, walk, dance, drum, and swim. Be aware of your feelings every minute of your life.

Protect Your Energy Field

The healing session will expose you to the dense emotions of fear, anger, resentment, and disharmony, among others. Your task is to maintain an inner milieu of unconditional loving and unconditional thinking so that you can assist your client in experiencing and expressing the pain underlying the emotions.

One way to ward off negative energy is to sustain the high rate of vibration generated by unconditional love. Toward this end, strive to regularly express gratitude, meditate, maintain a positive attitude, eat healthy foods, and avoid people, places, and events that dim your light. Remember that nothing can enter an energy field that is already full.

Another approach is to surround yourself with a bubble of intense white light. Envision a light so intense that only energies aligned with God's will, God's love, God's truth, and God's wisdom can survive in its presence. Now place around this bubble a metallic shield capable of repelling the most intense negativity.

THE HEALING SESSION

No healing session is like any other. Nor is it possible to predict where the silent voice of spirit will lead you. The following guidelines are offered as a blueprint to acquaint you with your general areas of responsibility.

Zeroing in on the Issues

If you are blessed with great clarity and an exquisite connection to your guides and teachers, you may be able to conduct an entire session without asking questions. If you are like most people, however, you will need to ask at least a few questions to zero in on the challenges to be addressed. Typical questions are "Why did you schedule this appointment?" "What would you like to gain from this session?" "Where in your body do you feel the energy blockage?" "How long has _____ been going on?" "What was going on in your life when it started?"

Your client's responses will help you proceed. Rely on your intuition to support you. Remain centered in unconditional loving and unconditional thinking throughout the session. For a description of the healing techniques that are most effective, see chapters 11, 12, and 13. Summaries of sample sessions appear in chapter 14.

Remaining Alert to Matching Pictures

A matching picture arises whenever a healer has an unresolved issue similar to the client's. A healer whose pain is triggered loses objectivity and compromises her ability to work with the client.

Any time you are caught in a matching picture, attempt to clear your energy field of the challenge by filling yourself with white light, regrounding yourself, and returning to an attitude of unconditional love. If the issue is too painful for you to clear your energy field, inform your client of the problem and apologize for not being able to offer assistance. Rather than leave your client alone midway through the process, recommend the services of another healer. Meanwhile, consider the triggering a gift to be reckoned with, and arrange to work through the underlying issue as soon as possible with a healer.

Rosalie's son, Mike, was electrocuted in 1977, at the age of fourteen. While working with clients whose children have died, she consciously steps back and raises her frequency. Only in this way can she rise above the matching picture of her own pain and loss.

Michael was emotionally incested by his mother and rejected by his father. Whenever he works with a client who has been emotionally abused or rejected by a parent, he takes a deep breath, disengages momentarily, and raises his vibration rate. He is then able to steer clear of the matching picture of his childhood.

Pacing the Session

Honor your client's tempo. Pay attention to his energy as well as his words. If he says, "Keep going—I'm fine," and you sense that he is not, proceed slowly. Pushing may only cause him to shut down.

Any time your client is resistant to continuing, ask if he would like some help. If he does, and you sense that his energy is aligned with his words, assist him. If he does not, shift your focus from clearing his energy field to exploring his resistance. You might ask, for example, "What is the benefit of staying stuck?" "What is your greatest fear about breaking free?" or "Would you prefer to come back and tackle this in another lifetime?" After breaking through his resistance, he will most likely be open to healing.

Evaluating When to End the Session

Our sessions normally last from an hour to an hour and a half. On rare occasions we have assisted a client for as long as two hours. Ultimately, the length of a session depends on the client's degree of openness, level of commitment to healing, and capacity to integrate change.

A session that extends beyond an hour and a half may signify that you are working with a highly resistant client. If so, he may not be at all receptive to your help. In fact, he may require a great deal of energy and, in return, minimize or resent your assistance. Highly resistant individuals are those who have perfected personality strategies that keep them identified with their limitations, and hence out of alignment with their essence. Working with them may not be in your best interest or theirs. For a description of resistant personality strategies, please see chapter 10.

The end of a session can be either time determined or process determined. Whichever approach you decide upon, be sure your client has completed the segment he began and that it has been woven into his soul purpose or life lessons. The more thorough the integration is, the more holding power the healing will have. If your preferred yardstick is time and several minutes remain, it is better to review the session than to start a new segment of work. If you are adhering more to process, end the session after completing an entire segment of work, as opposed to an individual piece. In either case, remain sensitive to your client's energy level; avoid overloading him by trying to accomplish too much.

Disconnecting and Cleansing

As the session draws to a close, disconnect from your client's energy field and return fully to your own. For this, you may either use a self-styled disengaging technique or silently repeat a form of identification that is unique to you, such as your telephone number or date of birth.

Next, cleanse your energy field and the energy in your work space. The act of cleansing can be as simple as washing your hands with soap and water while imagining that you are purging yourself and the environment of all negativity. Or light a white candle and envision it burning up the negativity in the room. Or place the palms of your hands on the floor to ground the negativity. Other grounding techniques, meditation, or centering will also help.

The objective is to sever the energy fields so that you will not absorb your client's pain, negative emotions, or illness. Incorporating the released energy will only render you ineffective and prevent your client from reclaiming his power, learning his life lessons, and taking action on significant issues in the days ahead.

Whose Responsibility Is This?

♦ It is the healer's responsibility to inform the client about fees for service before the session.

♦ It is the client's responsibility to provide payment at the end of the session.

♦ It is the healer's responsibility to maintain confidentiality.

♦ It is the client's responsibility to exercise discretion and accountability when sharing information outside of the session.

♦ It is the healer's responsibility to be grounded in loving energies, maintain a steady frequency, and invite the participation of the client's essence.

♦ It is the client's responsibility to decide how vulnerable to be.

♦ It is the healer's responsibility to provide information about soul purpose, soul qualities, life lessons, personality aspects, and the client's placement on the soul continuum.

♦ It is the client's responsibility to honor the integrity of the experience.

- It is the healer's responsibility to facilitate, with the client's permission, the release of suppressed emotions.
- It is the client's responsibility to be truthful and to feel the emotions.

- It is the healer's responsibility to disengage from a battle of wills.
- It is the client's responsibility to transcend habitual patterns of behavior.

- It is the healer's responsibility to honor the client's level of commitment to healing and to avoid working harder than the client.
- It is the client's responsibility to decide how committed to be.

- It is the healer's responsibility to end the session when the work is complete.
- It is the client's responsibility to provide the determining feedback.

- It is the healer's responsibility to assist in the integration of insights gleaned in the session.
- It is the client's responsibility to integrate the information.

- It is the healer's responsibility to furnish after-care suggestions.
- It is the client's responsibility to practice self-care.

TIPS FOR WORKING WITH A PARTNER

Collaborating with a partner, especially one of the opposite sex, provides an opportunity to combine your healing gifts with those based on a different set of experiences and perspectives. Aligned with your partner, you will magnify the love, sensitivity, and support that goes out to your client. This is particularly helpful while working with survivors of abuse.

The first order of business is to choose your partner wisely. As author Sam Keen says: There are only three questions you need to know the answer to. Who am I? Where am I going? And, after you have answered these two, Who is going with me? In deciding who is going with you, rely on your powers of discernment—the inner knowing that takes you beyond thought and illusion to absolute certainty.

There are several ways to maximize the potential of your healing partnership. For one, be sure a member of the team disengages at appropriate times. One of you can disengage from dialoguing, for example, and move into a state of relaxed awareness to obtain information about the deeper meaning of the issue under discussion. Later, while one of you assists the client in resolving an issue, the other can disengage to support the client's soul qualities, or to track the underlying cause of his resistance. If unresolved conflicts are projected onto one of you, the other can serve as a "fair witness," helping the client recognize the projection. When a client is experiencing denial, you can double the opportunities for a reality check.

The team approach can also overcome resistance. On several occasions, we have been guided to disengage from a client and strengthen the energetic love net between us by sending a ray of love, heart-to-heart, to each other. After increasing the love vibration between us, we surrounded the client with our enhanced energy. Many times this is all that is needed to dissolve resistance.

To take further advantage of your healing partnership, review your sessions together. Reflecting on a session with a colleague who was present promotes support, ongoing learning, and increased proficiency.

Tips for Working with a Translator

In times of emotional stress, clients who are multilingual will often revert to their native language to the point of being unable to comprehend your words. It is therefore a good idea to use a translator when working with people who speak a foreign language. The translator's job is twofold: to stay focused on you—speaking with the same tone, inflection, pace, and intensity—and to communicate your client's responses.

Inform each translator you work with that bonding with the client, getting lost in the client's story, or trying to protect the client or second-guess you is apt to undermine the success of the session. Also explain that any time the translator is in doubt about what to do, it is best to disengage from the client and look to you for guidance.

The delay involved in translating will alter the pace of the session. To prevent complications, allow the translator to decide how much of the dialogue can be comfortably translated. Also agree in advance on basic hand signals to indicate "stop," "speed up," and "slow down."

$\mathcal{T}en$

SIGNPOSTS OF RESISTANCE

* *

"If your heart is closed, you are closed to your soul."

—Don and Linda Pendleton

E VERY NOW AND THEN you will encounter a client who is highly resistant to healing. In the healing session, as in everyday life, these people will consciously or unconsciously act out a personality strategy that keeps them identified with their learned limitations. Such individuals may not be ready to trade in their personality aspects for soul qualities. Following are the most common tactics of resistance and some profiles of the people who hide behind them.

POWERLESSNESS

Unwillingness to accept information—Hiding behind a guise of powerlessness, these people become confused, argue, and diminish the validity of the information given to them, or they divert the dialogue by focusing on irrelevant issues. Used as a strategy, confusion prevents the client from making decisions that might upset others or disrupt the status quo. When confusion manifests, you will need to determine whether your client has made a breakthrough and is on new, uncharted ground or is merely refusing to take action.

Use of the conditional "Yes, but"—These people will appear to agree with you, then negate their concurrence. Regardless of the number of positive suggestions or the amount of support you give them, their response will be conditional, sabotaging both themselves and those who try to help them.

Jean, an actress in her late forties, complained about being exhausted. In response to each option we presented, she said yes, then proceeded to tell us why it would not work. For example, when we suggested that she cut back on some of her activities and take more time for herself, she said: "Yes. You are absolutely right! I should do that, but I can't, because everyone needs me and I can't let them down now, can I?"

Pleasing others—These people readily say yes, yet take no action. They fear that by committing to their own well-being they will lose the love of others. They may go from one healer to the next, seeking help yet never activating the suggestions they are given. When confronted, they may agree with you, refuse to take action, and be silently upset upon leaving the session.

Discounting oneself—These people have many excuses for not taking action—among them, "I am too old and it really doesn't matter anyway," "I'm in a relationship and my partner won't support me if I change," and "What would my children think?" When you encourage them to act on their newly gained insights, they will often reply, "I just can't."

Blaming others or life circumstances—Intent on judging others, these people complain about family, friends, and business associates. They may describe a litany of woes, attempting to win you over to reinforce their "Isn't it awful?" reality. Blaming others, including you, exempts them from having to initiate change. No matter how you try to clarify their predicament or explain the freedom available in taking responsibility for their actions, they will not give up their victim role.

Playing hostage to a personality groove—These people continually fall prey to a deeply ingrained pattern of behavior. Even when they are aware of their self-destructive cycle, they fail to realize that they can break it. Indeed, the longer the pattern remains in place, the more difficult it is to break. One client of ours openly admitted: "I've been at a decision point five times in recent years. I go so far and then stop myself from going further. I am not willing to risk my security." What was once an issue has become an impenetrable barrier. No matter what you say or do, these people will not give themselves permission to break free.

OVERASSERTION OF POWER AND CONTROL

Insisting on doing it alone—Hiding behind their perceived sense of power and control, these people believe they have to work in isolation and do everything themselves. Given input that can both ease and speed up their process, they opt for the long, hard road. Michael once had a business partner who refused his advice, saying: "I cannot benefit from your assistance and take giant leaps forward. I have to go through each step myself and make all the mistakes. How else am I going to learn the ropes?" Soon afterward, the business failed.

Fear of being out of control—These people believe that to ensure their safety they must maintain absolute control of themselves, others, and their environment. They fear that if they let go of the reins they will either fall apart, die, or succumb to destruction. Their need to control is so consuming that they do not allow themselves to relax, receive support, or feel vulnerable. To them, vulnerability is synonymous with weakness.

Frances, a financial advisor in her mid-forties, complained throughout our session about the "cold air" in the room, the "excessive amount of light" coming through the window, even the candle burning in the corner. She requested a blanket and a pillow, then objected to the "noise" emanating from the heater. Regardless of what we said or did, she resisted our help. Finally, she told us that if we were better healers we would lead her to her emotions, and that she knew we didn't like her, couldn't wait for the session to end, and agreed to see her only because we wanted the money.

When we confronted her about her projection, she replied: "I do that to healers all the time. Tell me something I don't know." The session lasted longer than usual, but despite our extra time together, she refused to take responsibility for changing her attitude toward us, herself, or her life.

Engaging in a battle of wills—These people like to outsmart the competition, because for them, being right is paramount. Admitting to a mistake or acknowledging that *you* are right is tantamount to suffering a defeat. Sometimes, they are simply exercising their strong wills; more often, they are flexing their opposition muscles because they have found that resistance is their sole source of power. If you become involved in a battle of wills, back off the moment you realize that you are working harder than your client.

John, a football coach in his early fifties, did everything he could to block our assistance. Despite the variety of approaches we used, he continued to avoid his feelings and refuse us entry into his energy field. Oddly enough, each time we started to back off, he would soften and reach out for help. As we refocused to assist him, however, his defenses would resurface. Suddenly, Michael backed off and Rosalie surrounded John with compassion, one of his soul qualities. Immediately, he relaxed and admitted that he was afraid to let go of control, because he might "hurt someone" or "destroy the planet."

Striving for expedience—These people do only what is convenient for them. They are not interested in being confronted or supported. Their focus is on being right and in control. This stance may place you in a double bind. There is little you can do, other than listen and offer suggestions, until they let go of needing to have their own way.

Shawn, a writer in his late forties, frequently received clear spiritual guidance, but he listened to his guides only when it suited him to do so. Any time they broached a fear-laden subject, he would block their communication. When we pointed out the yes-no dance he was performing, he said his guides were too demanding and he did not trust them. Aware of a split between his allegiance to personal will and his desire to follow inner guidance, we asked him if his guidance was grounded in love. He said yes and reminded us that he had acted upon it when he agreed with it. We explained that the choice was his and we were not invested in convincing him to listen to his guides. He crossed his arms and legs, smiled smugly, and said, "Good."

FAILURE TO COMMUNICATE

Shrouded by a cloak of silence, these people have hidden agendas and expect others to read their minds. They also hold undisclosed expectations and either consciously or unconsciously hope to have them understood. When their expectations are not met, these people become angry and resentful. Failure to communicate is prevalent among those raised in dysfunctional families.

Karen, a seriously ill office manager in her late forties, complained that her husband never communicated with her. We asked her several times if she had expressed her feelings to him. Each time, she replied belligerently, saying, "He should know by now," "It's obvious," and "No matter how much I try to communicate, he doesn't respond." Regardless of the approach we took, she failed to acknowledge the part she played in the communication bottleneck affecting her marriage and her health.

SPIRITUAL BYPASS

Hiding behind a screen of feigned spirituality, these people deny their pain, anger, or other unresolved emotional issues. They rhapsodize about how great life is, the beauty in everyone, the importance of affirming only positive, loving thoughts and feelings. Many even believe they have moved toward a state of forgiveness, when in reality they have not yet dealt with their suppressed feelings. These people excel in the art of spiritual bypass.

Richard, a former government employee in his mid-forties, had been fired from his job, abandoned by his lover of twenty years, hit hard financially, and compelled to forfeit the home he had spent ten years designing. When we offered to work with him, he claimed that his life was wonderful, the gods were with him, and he had no problems.

Avoidance of Feelings

Philosophizing—Hiding behind a philosophical orientation, these thinkers are either unwilling or unable to get in touch with their emotions, or even their physical sensations. They like to begin sentences with "I think," "I think I feel," or "I feel that—." They prefer the safety of figuring things out and ruminating on life, as opposed to delving into their emotions. Unless these individuals permit themselves to experientially differentiate a feeling from a thought, they will continue in the avoidance mode.

Etherealizing—These people refuse to fully enter their physical bodies, and often, the earthly dimension. They have judged the earth experience and its people as inferior, and seem to be biding their time till they can go back "home." Many take pride in their resistance. Ironically, those who excel in the art of avoiding their humanness fail to realize that the only way to complete their earth stay is by fully experiencing the lessons they have committed to learning. By avoiding these, they are only ensuring another return to this dimension.

Paula, by age forty-two, had been to many healers and prided herself on being "so unique" that nobody could help her. She scheduled an appointment with us even though she doubted we could assist her. As we started to work with her, neither of us could read her energy or elicit an emotional response from her. After disengaging, we learned from our guides that only 30 percent of Paula's energy was in her body. When we shared this information with her, she openly expressed her disdain for humanity. She was affiliated with space beings and had come to earth to learn about the human experience, she confessed, but was unwilling to give it a try.

We told Paula that to continue her work with us she would have to agree to be more fully in her human body. At that moment, we noticed that her brow chakra—the dwelling place of the third eye and center for psychic sight—was blocked. We recognized the blockage as a sign that she had either experienced or committed an act so terrible she did not want to remember it. Despite our offers to help her fulfill her soul purpose, she refused to be more present in her body and resisted further help.

Fantasizing—These people, fearful of embracing their emotional realities, create a fantasy life that they project to the world. They cannot bear to face the truth, and will even create an emotional or physical crisis to avoid such a confrontation. They may use all their resources to convince you to agree with their false sense of reality. The underlying self-deception may not even become evident when they look inside themselves to see if the way they are living is in alignment with their soul purpose and life lessons.

Trevor, an interior designer in his mid-thirties, came to us because he thought he was going crazy and wanted information about his soul purpose. He seemed depressed and complained that his marriage was falling apart. He and his wife had separated many times, he explained, but he was unable to build a life for himself without his family. When he learned that he was in a practice lifetime and his soul purpose was to explore autonomy, he said he had no idea how to do that.

Although Trevor had known for years that his marriage was over, he had lied to himself and others, because he could not face the consequences of divorce. The breakup of his relationship was so terrifying to him that he created a series of financial, emotional, and physical crises to prevent his wife from leaving. He even tried to engage our support for his fantasy of a marriage that would work.

Projecting—These people wholeheartedly believe that others are the source of their unhappiness, which is in fact rooted in their own unexplored feelings about a past injury. The unresolved issues are projected onto individuals who trigger the original feelings, usually because they have traits in common with the perpetrator. People who project are unconsciously replicating painful situations from the past, all the while mistaking present-day events for unexamined past traumas.

Tina, a recent college graduate in her early twenties, had been dominated by her father. Upon entering the business world, she began projecting her unresolved father issues onto her employer, recapitulating the sense of inadequacy she had felt as a child. During the healing session, she refused to listen to Michael's suggestions and accused him of not understanding her. Rosalie—epitomizing the compassionate, nurturing mother figure—received Tina's positive projections.

Overidentification with Feelings

Identifying completely with feelings of impotence—These people have not worked out their feelings of futility and powerlessness, and react strongly to individuals who have taken charge of their lives, including a healer of the same sex as the person with whom they have unfinished issues. In addition, they have learned to cope without addressing their problems. When you help these people touch their pain, their accumulated emotion may be unleashed at you. Beware—these individuals can be ruthless in their vengeance!

Tanya, an airline stewardess in her mid-thirties, seemed excited to heal and was easily able to access her emotions. Her life had been punctuated by failure—a marginal income, no intimate relationship, an addiction to alcohol, and other disappointments. We worked with her on several occasions, until one day her anger and rage toward her father, and men in general, blazed out at Michael. Determined to get even with her father, she seemed to be saying, "The only way I can win and be safe is if you lose."

Behaving like a trauma-drama king or queen—These people live in a perpetual state of crisis, attracting attention and deriving their identity from an endless succession of catastrophes. Regardless of how much help and support they receive, they find a way to stage another drama. Bored with healthy relationships, they seek out stressful situations to satisfy their need for emotional excitement. The addiction to drama and the rush it produces is similar to the dependence others have on alcohol or drugs.

Identifying completely with a disease or illness—These people, who normally have few social skills, hold on to their symptoms as though their lives depended on them. They use illness as a means for obtaining love and attention, project a "poor, helpless me" image, and expect others to take care of them. Although they consult with healers, they are ambivalent about being healthy and usually play out their favorite form of "I've got you" with the therapist. Such clients have come to us saying, "No one has ever been able to help me, and I'm sure you can't either, but I'll give it one last chance." Be vigilant—these people are skillful at soliciting fee reductions, extra time, and unlimited attention. They often become professional patients and energy suckers.

Charlotte, a graphic artist in her early fifties, called for an appointment, saying, "I'm sure you've heard of me. I'm the chronic fatigue (ME) person." Before we had a chance to ask questions, she proceeded to tell us that nobody had been able to help her, she didn't believe in energy work, and she resented being told that she created her illness. She also explained that her debilitating condition had developed when her husband of twenty-five years left her for a younger woman and that she had no transportation, could not climb stairs, was available only at certain times, and had no money. We immediately concluded that she was not committed to her own healing and suggested that she consult with someone who could see her on an ongoing basis.

Rigid Belief in Long-term Therapy

People with a predisposing belief that healing takes a long time discount quick and easy interventions. Many have invested dozens of years and thousands of dollars in their search for relief. In fact, most of their day-to-day undertakings are focused on their pain.

Beth, a part-time college student in her mid-thirties, had spent at least five years and thousands of dollars seeking an understanding of her condition. Despite extensive efforts, she was barely able to hold her life together. When we tuned into her soul purpose—the use of balanced intuition—she responded with tears and proceeded to recall times in which she had violated her intuition. At the end of the session, she discounted all her release work, because she doubted that her energy field could have cleared so quickly.

Martyrdom

Doing penance—Believing that they were sent to earth as a punitive measure, these people blindly accept that their role here is to suffer and remain ignorant of other options. Most martyrs complain. Many become ill because they have exhausted themselves taking care of others, if not "the world." Some are so dedicated to their suffering that they do not complain. Several organized religions support their zeal by espousing that the only way to get close to God is by suffering. (Check for old vows!)

Steven, a successful businessman in his mid-forties, could not find satisfaction in an intimate relationship. On the surface, he seemed committed to his healing. In a discussion about life and risk-taking, however, he became cynical and alluded to the earth as a penitentiary. He suspected he had done something wrong and had been sent here to do penance. His negativity and distrust of people, which had destroyed many potentially long-term relationships, was also subverting his pledge to healing.

Self-sacrificing—These people are so busy rushing around taking care of others that they fail to set aside the time needed to complete their own healing process. During a session, they do not appear to be highly resistant. Afterward, however, they refuse to carve out time to reflect on the session and integrate the changes it elicited. Their sacrificial lifestyle short-circuits much of the work they accomplish.

Part 4
ADVANCED HEALING TECHNIQUES

Eleven

HEALING TECHNIQUES TO USE IN EVERY SESSION

• • • • • • • • • • • • • • • • •

"Love is reason. Everything else is an excuse."

—Alan Cohen

THE SOUL EMPOWERMENT approach to healing calls for techniques that on the surface may appear simple. Yet in practice, the energetic shifts they produce are profound. When the healing room fills with spirit beings and the energy is felt by nearly everyone present, it will be impossible to question the multidimensional support that is available to you as you become an instrument of healing.

The techniques that follow will help you engage the assistance of this ever-ready support system. Incorporate these techniques into every session you conduct. More specialized tools are addressed in the next chapter.

FOCUSED INTENTION

Focusing the conscious mind creates a powerful energy field that attracts the resources and information needed to facilitate a healing. To begin, invite your personality to step aside, and connect with your faith in the ongoing availability of guidance as you work with your client. Focus your intention by activating as many senses as possible so that you can see, hear, and feel the results you desire. Make sure that your will is aligned with God's and that what you are seeking is in the highest and best interest of everyone concerned. Using your will to overpower a client generates karma; using it to merge with the client's energy field promotes healing.

INVOKING SPIRIT GUIDES

Spirit is always available to help, most often in the form of guides and teachers. You, as well as each of your clients, has guides and teachers. They come from many dimensions and include devas, elementals, inner earth beings, angels, and space beings. Remember that your relationship with these beings is reciprocal: They offer their assistance, and you honor their presence by making decisions that empower your soul. For this reason, be sure to invite in only guides and teachers that are in alignment with your essence.

Your first task is to prepare to receive information. Your second is to help your client take action. If either one of you fails to act upon the messages delivered, your guides will eventually withdraw, leaving you to operate under your own power and, in the process, casting you back from soul empowerment to personality empowerment.

At the beginning of each session, invite the assistance of your spirit guides as well as those of your client. Also call upon your soul affiliations and those of your client. Soul affiliations will support you by stabilizing your soul frequency. In addition you may wish to summon all the energies of evolution that have made a commitment to serve the well-being of the planet and her people. Close each session by thanking the guides for their assistance and requesting that the healing angels continue to work with your client in the days to come.

DIALOGUING

Dialoguing gives voice to painful blocked memories and brings the suppressed feelings to the surface, where they can be worked with, healed, and integrated. Your job is to present open-ended statements that will steer the client toward an awareness of the root cause of his dilemma. Your client's job is to relax and complete each statement with the first response that comes to mind.

You might say, for example: "Try your best to fill in the blanks in the following statements. 'The benefit I get out of being confused (sick, in pain, in grief) is _____.' 'If my mind (stomach, back, heart) could speak, it would tell you _____.'" Repeat each unfinished statement until the response feels complete.

The degree of emotional release accompanying your client's responses will reveal the intensity of the trauma trapped in his body. (*Note:* This technique will also clarify personality issues that are disrupting your client's alignment with his soul purpose. Your objective, however, is to go beyond the personal issues and family beliefs that form the content of his life, and focus on the soul purpose and soul qualities that form its context.)

CLAPPING

This is one of the quickest and most effective ways of releasing blocked energy and of clearing out negative energy associated with an issue, attitude, or belief system. While clapping, remember to use focused intention, concentrating on the outcome you desire. The sound of the clap will let you know whether or not the energy is being discharged. A sharp, solid clap indicates that it is; a clap that sounds flat, dull, or hollow indicates that it is not. (*Note:* Avoid clapping while your client is integrating the healing, or you may sabotage the process.)

To release blocked energy, have your client close his eyes and imagine a loosening of the blockage and a release of the energy. When you intuitively sense that he is ready, focus your intention on releasing the blocked energy, then clap as loud as possible near the affected area of his body, coming as close as you can without touching him. Surprise is a key factor, so make sure your client has his eyes closed and does not anticipate the clap. (This approach is also effective for cutting psychic cords, as described below, and for releasing entities, as discussed in chapter 13.)

To clear out negative energy, have your client, with eyes closed, gather all the negative energy he feels and focus it into a tight ball about 6 inches (15 cm) in front of his third eye. Ask him to repeat this gathering process several times until he feels that all the negative energy has been transferred from his body to the ball. Then have him concentrate on consolidating and compressing it into an even tighter ball. When he is least expecting it, clap your hands as loud as you can in the area of the energy ball.

Harry, a dentist in his mid-twenties, complained of a recurring pain in his upper back. He described himself as an extrovert who was enjoying life and had no idea what was causing his pain. As we worked with Harry, he spoke of feeling "held back," as though his hands and feet were somehow restrained. While listening to his description, we both received a past-life image of him with his hands and feet chained to a prison wall. He, too, could sense a lifetime of restricted freedom.

We asked Harry if he was willing to let us help him, and he said he was. We then imagined shackles encircling his hands and feet. Using the technique of clapping, we energetically broke the holding pattern of the bolts and pulled apart the shackles from his hands and feet. Harry, for the first time in his conscious memory, felt freedom of movement in his limbs. His back pain disappeared within minutes.

CUTTING PSYCHIC CORDS

Psychic cords are energy attachments that have formed between an individual and people with whom he has interacted, as well as places he has frequented. Some cords are benign; most, however, were set in place by people attempting to influence, control, or dominate him. These cords are attached to one or more of the chakras, or points of energy in the auric field that correspond to places in the body. From there, they pull on the person much like marionette strings pull on a puppet. They can affect one's clarity of thinking, physical health, emotional well-being, and even psychic knowing.

Cords are frequently found between family members, lovers, and business affiliates, as well as associates from former lifetimes.

Although it is helpful to know when and why these cords were created, it is more important to sever them. Your mission is to detect these cords, inform your client of their implications, and ask his permission to sever them. Cutting the cords will allow him to be free in his own energy field.

You can be almost certain that a cord exists if your client is overly affected by another individual. To double check, ask him whether or not he is corded. If he says he is, see if he wishes to have the cord severed. If he agrees, ask him to close his eyes, visualize the area of attachment, and describe how the cord affects him. Then have him imagine the release of the cord. You can assist by clapping loudly near the area of attachment.

Susan, after forty years of marriage, was in her second year of widowhood. She talked frequently to her deceased husband and often felt his presence nearby. Although she had started to date, she would not allow herself to love another man for fear of betraying her husband. During our session, she was overtly emotional and reported that she was still grief stricken. The intensity of her emotions, combined with the fact that she could still feel her former husband's energy around her, strongly suggested the existence of a cord.

After consulting our guides, we reminded Susan that her soul purpose was to practice loving. We then explained that her refusal to continue loving was holding back both her and her deceased husband who, similarly corded, was unable to evolve along his soul path. When we asked her if there was an energetic connection between her deceased husband and herself, she identified one cord attached to her heart and another fastened to her root chakra, in the sacral-coccyx region between her legs. We invited her to call back the energies of her deceased husband and ask him whether or not he supported her in loving another man and thereby realigning with her soul commitment. She did, then crying and clutching her heart, she told us that he wanted her to move on and continue loving.

When they completed their interaction, we asked Susan if she was ready to let the cords go. She agreed, whereupon we had her close her eyes, take a deep breath, and at the count of three, exhale quickly, releasing the cord to her heart. Just as she began exhaling, Michael clapped loudly, close to her heart center. They repeated this sequence of events with the second cord. Soon after opening her eyes, Susan reported that she could feel a difference.

FORGIVING

A client who has been hurt or abused will carry feelings of anger and resentment. These feelings will produce negative energy as well as energetic breaks in her auric field. Strong negative thoughts or feelings about someone can also promote the growth of psychic cords that will bind your client to her abuser. To make matters worse, she will continue to suffer, whereas her abuser will have long since forgotten the incident. She will carry the toxic energy until she succeeds in releasing it through forgiveness.

Forgiveness does not condone a harmful act or relieve the offender of responsibility for the abuse. Rather, it frees the client so she can truly live her life. Forgiveness entails renouncing judgments and the desire for revenge, affirming the perfection of the offender's essence, and relinquishing all perceptions of the offender's personality limitations. You can go a step further by asking God, the Great Spirit, or your client's Higher Power to heal the situation. In the end, forgiveness is extended for indiscretions and errors committed not only against others but against oneself.

When a client's emotions are either strongly expressed or deeply suppressed, it may be necessary to guide her back to an earlier age or even a past lifetime so she can revisit the painful scene, review the experience, and reevaluate the decisions she made at that time. In such instances, use visualization techniques to call forth the energy of the offender, or to assemble the group of people who were present at the scene. Then invite your client to dialogue with them as if they were physically present. This technique is extremely useful when dealing with an offender who is deceased or the resolution of a past-life trauma.

Finally, have your client repeat the following affirmations.

Forgiveness Affirmations

I (client's name), from the essence of my being, now forgive everyone who has ever hurt me on any level, in any way from the beginning of time. I absolutely and totally forgive them right now! I especially extend my loving forgiveness to _____.

I (client's name), from the essence of my being, now ask for forgiveness from everyone I have ever hurt on any level, in any way from the beginning of time. I absolutely and totally ask for forgiveness right now! I especially request loving forgiveness from _____.

I (client's name), from the essence of my being, now forgive myself for all the pain and suffering I have caused myself on any level, in any way since the beginning of time. I absolutely and totally forgive myself right now! I especially forgive myself for _____.

BREAKING OLD VOWS

A client who has taken oaths or made vows, and failed to break them after completing the experiences, has attachments in his energy field. These energetic attachments, unless they are in alignment with his essence, will stir up problems from one lifetime to the next, until they are broken. The most common culprits are vows of poverty, celibacy, allegiance, invisibility, service, obedience, silence, pain, lack, suffering, giving away one's power, and loyalty (to an order, family, relationship, or job).

Although the original vows were in alignment with your client's soul purpose at the time, now, perhaps centuries later, they are not. Only by breaking the old vows will the individual be free to live in alignment with his current soul purpose and life lessons.

To assist a client in breaking vows, begin by explaining: "Because neither one of us is wise enough to know which vows are to be broken and which ones are to be kept, we must ask God to take charge. We will say the words, and spirit will do the work!" Then have your client repeat the following sequence. This invocation is extremely powerful when recited in a group setting.

Vow Breaking Sequence

I (client's name) now break all vows, promises, and commitments I have ever made—on any level, in any way from the beginning of time—that no longer serve my present soul purpose. I especially break all vows of poverty, celibacy, pain, lack, suffering, powerlessness, silence, obedience, and invisibility. I now give myself absolute and total permission to follow my soul's true path.

If your client is aware of specific vows, add, "I also break my vows of _____."

CALLING BACK SOUL QUALITIES

In this lifetime as well as others, clients who have judged or condemned aspects of their soul essence have cast them out of their being. Wholeness cannot be achieved until these soul qualities are reintegrated. A man who has abused his power and sworn never to touch it again, for example, can heal by forgiving himself and embracing his power once again.

Aspects that are typically judged and sent away include creativity, sensitivity, sensuality, sexuality, clarity, risk-taking, and commitment. (See page 45 for a more complete listing of soul qualities.) In each case, calling the soul quality back promotes wholeness.

To assist a client in calling back aspects of himself that are currently scattered throughout the universes, have him repeat the following two sequences. This exercise is extremely powerful when recited in a group setting.

Energy Clearing Sequence

I (client's name), from the essence of my being, now command all energies and entities that are not aligned with divine essence and my soul purpose to be blessed and be gone right now! I ask the angels to take these energies skyward to the schools of wisdom, where they may be honored for what they have learned and what they have taught.

Soul Quality Retrieval Sequence

I (client's name), from the essence of my soul, now command all aspects of my soul essence that I have scattered throughout the universes to return to me right now! I especially call back my soul qualities of strength, courage, power, joy, happiness, love, passion, health, abundance, and others that support my soul's empowerment.

Invite your client to add other qualities he wishes to reclaim. Then encourage him to breathe in all the restored qualities and to feel them as they return. Finally have him continue the sequence.

I (client's name) fill myself with my own essence and joyfully take full responsibility for this vehicle called my physical body right now!

Twelve

ADDITIONAL HEALING TECHNIQUES

* *

"Luck is just another word for God."

—Old Hindu Saying

HEALING IS LIMITED only by the imagination. Whatever we conceive of and then activate through our focused intention becomes manifest in one of the many dimensions in our midst. The following techniques employ the more subtle energies. Effective use of their healing potential hinges on an unwavering trust in yourself and in spirit.

AURA CLEANSING

The aura is a subtle energy field that surrounds all matter, including people, animals, trees, plants, rocks, and water. Although invisible to most people it is as real as the physical body. The body's aura is much like the atmosphere of the earth, growing progressively thinner the farther out it goes. It is alive, sensitive, and easily affected by slight shifts in the person's attitude, mode of thinking or feeling, actions, and eating habits. A person who is positive and healthy will have a strong, bright, vibrant energy field that expands outward from the body. Someone who is negative or sick will have a weak, dull auric field that contracts inward toward the body.

People who can perceive the human aura describe it as egg shaped, colorful, and aglow at each of the chakras. The colors of the aura change constantly in response to alterations in thoughts, feelings, and actions.

Illness and disease can be detected in the auric field years before they manifest in the physical body. The reason is that at the onset of trauma or influx of negativity, the auric field is the first area affected. Healing, to be effective, must therefore extend to this subtle energy field.

The best disease preventative is frequent cleansing of the auric field. Cleansing the aura is much like brushing down a large animal, such as a horse. First, be sure to ground yourself and focus your mind on the results you hope to achieve. Then imagine that attached to the palms of your hands are large brushes capable of clearing the aura of all negativity.

To do a general aura cleansing, hold your hands close together, palms outward, and, facing your client, move them from her head to her feet, keeping them about 6 inches (15 cm) away from her body. After sweeping the "brushes" down her body and over the tops of her feet, allow them to touch the floor to ground out any negative energy. Moving clockwise, repeat this movement down the right side of her body. Proceed until you have completed all four sides. (For more detailed instructions on removing negativity from the human aura, please see Michael's book on healing energy.)

When working on a particular part of the body that has been affected by trauma, move from the trunk to the extremities, using the same technique. Repeat the cleansing two or three times, or until you feel the energy field is clear. Because trauma is seldom experienced in only one part of the body, it is a good idea to follow up any localized healing work with a general aura cleansing.

SEALING THE AURA

After a healing session or an aura cleansing, be sure to protect the aura from negativity by sealing it. The purpose of sealing the aura is much like that of stitching a person up after surgery.

Once again, begin with focused intention. Then, imagining that your hands have special aura-sealing abilities, or are able to emit a protective salve, sweep them slowly from your client's head to her feet, without touching her body. Move clockwise as before, until you have sealed all four sides of her auric field. This protection will most likely last for at least a few hours.

Shirley, a hotel manager in her late fifties, had a recurring pain in her right foot, which began soon after an operation she underwent six years earlier. Although she had returned to the surgeon and conferred with other medical professionals to find out the cause of her pain, no one was able to help her. After we cleansed and sealed the energy field around her foot, which took only a few minutes, she sighed in relief. The pain was gone.

Allen, a young teenager, had a bad accident and was taken to the hospital for X-rays. Although he had broken no bones, he was seriously bruised and in considerable pain. Working with his energy field, we removed the trauma and pain, then sealed his energy field. When he awoke the next morning, his pain was gone and there were no black-and-blue marks. He felt good enough to go to work.

Reaching in and Pulling out Blocked Energy

This technique alleviates pain, illness, and trauma, including past-life distress related to an old wound caused by a dagger, sword, firearm, or other weapon. It requires the use of a physical hand or its "etheric double" to remove blocked energy originating in the present or a past lifetime. To envision your hand's etheric double, imagine a glove-shaped energy field surrounding your real hand and able to enter any area of the body you wish to reach. When removing objects that extend outward from the body, use your physical hand; to remove those lodged within the body, use your etheric hand. In either case, the energy trapped in the body will give way as you reach in and pull it out.

Begin by asking your client's permission to eliminate the blockage. Invite him to imagine the process with you, and whenever possible, follow his guidance. With each movement you make to release the blocked energy, ask your client what he is feeling. After the object is removed, cleanse his auric field.

Helen, a botanist in her late forties, came to us for healing soon after her physician had diagnosed a tumor in her throat. First we had her break the vows from past lives, participate in dialoguing to identify reasons for the blockage, and verbalize her unspoken feelings. Then, to speed the healing process, we used the etheric energy of our hands, combined with focused intention, to reach into the area containing the tumor and remove both the negative energy and the cancerous cells. The following week X-rays showed no sign of a tumor.

Henry, a radio broadcaster in his late forties, had a recurring pain in his right side. He had been to several medical professionals to find the cause of the problem, with no success. As a last resort, he came to us. After helping him break the vows from past lives and using the dialogue technique to arrive at reasons for the blockage, we had Henry relax and imagine the cause of the pain. He soon felt a long, round piece of wood in his side. Tracking this sensation, he realized it was the pointed head of an arrow. As he connected with his memories of the initial wound, his pain increased. Using the etheric energy of our hands, combined with focused intention, we were able to reach in and remove the arrowhead, as well as the trauma that had been locked in his body. When the excision was complete, his pain vanished.

HEALING SPLITS

A split is a break in thinking that has produced an imbalanced energy field. Its cause is an either-or perspective leaving no middle ground between such notions as head/heart, teacher/student, masculine/ feminine, divine love/personal love, or creativity/practicality. Its primary characteristics are a feeling of inner emptiness and an inability to flow freely with choices.

Balancing Split Energies

An effective way to heal a split is to invite your client to sit and place her hands on her legs, palms open and facing upward. Encourage her to sense both aspects of the split. Once she is able to feel the two qualities, ask her which one wants to be in her right hand and which one wants to be in her left hand.

Focusing on her right hand, have her call forth the energy of the quality it is holding. Ask her to become acquainted with this energy as if meeting a new person. Then have her explain why the energy is needed and, if necessary, apologize for having judged it. Invite her to thank the energy for coming. Repeat the procedure, focusing on her left hand.

Next, lead your client through the following integration sequence. Have her close her eyes and extend her arms, shoulder-height, out to the sides, palms facing forward. Ask her to imagine her hands as giant magnets that, attracting each other, will come together in such a way that the two energies will blend into one. As her hands come together, have her breathe more deeply to integrate the merging. Encourage her to feel the integration and to bring her hands to her heart, breathing in the healing of the split. Allow time for her to absorb the integration.

To anchor the experience in your client's consciousness, invite her to ask her heart for a symbol, word, sound, or color. Remind her that she will be able to reinforce this solidarity of opposites any time she wishes by remembering the integration symbol.

Cynthia, a loan officer in her late thirties, came to us with her seventeen-year-old daughter Paula, who had been diagnosed as schizophrenic. While working with Paula, we learned that her problems had begun soon after the divorce of her parents, eight years before. At the time, Paula was living part-time with her mother and the rest of the time with her father. To please her mother, she developed one set of personality traits, including behaviors, communication styles, interests, and even dietary preferences. To please her father, she formed an entirely different set.

To heal the split and assist in Paula's return to authenticity, we guided her to blend her two ways of being into one. When she had integrated the twin sets of behaviors, we advised her to tell her parents the truth—that all this time she had sacrificed who she was for who she thought they each wanted her to be. We also had her ask them if they would continue to love her if she let go of pleasing them. When they independently realized the dynamics their daughter had been playing out since the divorce, they were relieved and excited to support her in her healing process.

Balancing Masculine and Feminine Energies

Nowhere but on planet earth is there a split between masculine and feminine. This division, like others, poses challenges and also provides tremendous learning opportunities.

For centuries, males were expected to be warriors and providers, while females served as mothers, wives, and nurturers. These role models have become so deeply ingrained in the human psyche that we tend to forget we actually possess a combination of masculine and feminine energies. Indeed, only when these two expressions of energy are in balance with each other are we whole and healthy.

Masculine energy is usually described as strong, intellectual, independent, assertive, focused, and action oriented. Healthy masculine energy uses its strength to protect, provide for, and manifest. When unbalanced by the feminine, it turns aggressive, abusive, or violent.

Feminine energy, at the other end of the polarity, is often portrayed as feeling, receptive, caring, and surrendering. Healthy feminine energy uses its receptivity to love, nurture, and support. When one-sided, it displays weakness, jealousy, seductiveness, or extreme emotionality.

Any time you are working with a client who has judged one or both of these energies, be on the lookout for a masculine-feminine split. In such instances, coming to terms with the judgment will depend on healing the split in the energy field.

Arthur, a graphic artist in his early thirties, had an attentive mother and an uncommunicative father. As much as he idolized his mother, he seethed with anger toward his father for not giving him love and attention. While growing up, Art developed the feminine qualities of sensitivity, and caretaking; however, he was unable to activate his masculine energy enough to support himself. We realized he had judged the feminine as good and the masculine as bad, and in so doing had sabotaged his potential for success. We assisted him in forgiving his father and in releasing his idealism toward his mother. We then healed the split in his energy field.

Tim, a real estate agent in his early forties, approached life through logic. He explained that he was petrified of losing control of his emotions. His mother, he said, was often hysterical, and as a young child he decided never to be like her. We assisted Tim in forgiving his mother and in making peace with his own sensitivity.

Sue, a receptionist in her mid-forties, had been physically and emotionally abused by her father. As a result, she became fearful of men and formed a negative opinion of masculine energy. Eventually, she was told she had a psychotic disorder and was placed on medication. When she came for healing two years later, she was having difficulty sleeping and was afraid no one would like her if she discontinued her medication.

During the healing, the right (masculine) side of her body began to shake, whereupon she explained that she was afraid to trust any masculinity, including her own. As we helped her make peace with her masculine energy, she calmed down and integrated her masculine and feminine sides. After the healing, she was able to ease off her medication and sleep peacefully at night.

INNER-CHILD INTEGRATION

This three-step technique is especially effective when used with people who are out of touch with their feelings. Begin by having your client either sit in a chair or lie face-up on a massage table.

1. **Sensing the inner child**—Ask your client to invite the energy of his inner child to communicate with him. Then have him extend his arms fully forward, as if he were picking up a young child. Ask if he can see, hear, feel, sense, or imagine this child in front of him. Have him describe the child in as much detail as possible. Then gently ask for more information: "How far

away is this inner child?" "How old is he?" "What is he wearing?" "What is he feeling?" "Is he happy or sad?" "What is he doing?" "What else can you tell me about the child and his needs?" The purpose of asking these questions is to deepen your client's sensory awareness of his inner child.

2. **Apologizing to the inner child**—Ask your client to apologize to his inner child for having abandoned him; to admit that life was scary at that time, so much so that he left the child behind because it was no longer safe to hold on to him; and to explain that he now realizes his mistake. Encourage your client to express appreciation to the child and say that he really loves him. Then have your client ask the child to forgive him and come back. Finally, have the child give voice to his needs, such as spontaneity, sensitivity, honesty, or attention.

3. **Reclaiming the inner child**—Encourage your client to ask the child if he would trust him enough to give him another chance. If the child appears hesitant, ask what he needs in order to feel safe again. Ask him to teach your client how they might learn and grow together. Encourage your client to listen patiently to the needs of this child. (*Note:* Never try to force, rush, or threaten the child. Instead, let your client acknowledge that he understands any lack of trust. He might even ask the child to visit from time to time so they can gradually reestablish a trusting relationship.)

   When the child agrees to return, have your client imagine taking him in his outstretched arms. Ask the child if he would like to be placed in your client's adult heart. Then invite him to slowly move his hands toward his chest until they are touching his heart.

This technique often stirs up suppressed emotions and tears, so be sure to allow quiet time for the integration. At the end of the exercise, gently ask your client how he feels now that he has recovered his inner child. Expressing his response will help solidify the experience in his conscious mind.

COMPLETION RITUAL

Any time you would like to help a client symbolically mark an ending, use this technique. Begin by having her tune into the feelings and emotions she wishes to release. Then ask her to imagine placing them all in a significant object or, in lieu of an object, a rock or piece of wood. After the session, have her ceremonialize her completion by taking action, such as throwing, burning, or burying the significant object or its replacement. For an alternative ceremony, she could burn a candle, release a balloon, write her feelings on a sheet of paper, or place flowers where the traumatic incident occurred.

In either case, while the release is taking place, encourage her to grieve. Afterward, remind her to fill herself up with white light, unconditional love, and her soul qualities.

CALLING BACK A GROUP

While working with a client who in a past lifetime was part of a group or religious order, it is sometimes appropriate to call back the energies of the other members. The presence of these energies is most helpful to clients who, still influenced by the memory of a past-life group, need to state a truth or ask questions or clear a judgment against themselves.

To begin, have your client close her eyes, move into a state of deep relaxation, and indicate whether or not she is willing to call back the original group. At first, she may be afraid or anxious; however, once she begins addressing the group, she is apt to find her fears ungrounded. Groups that are called back tend to be gentle, forgiving, and eager to have the person engage in self-forgiveness and move on. (*Note:* Clients who were members of strict religious orders are usually told that most members of the order have advanced their development and that remaining loyal to old vows holds back the evolution of the group.)

Phil, a spiritual teacher in his early forties, was obsessed with being well grounded. He told us he was terrified of becoming so powerful he would disappear! As we worked together, we learned of a lifetime in which he had taught a group about energy and one day merged with the energy, transforming into pure light. Unable to return to his physical body, he judged himself for having let his students down.

After calling back the souls of his students, we had him ask if they resented him. They said no and explained that they were grateful for his demonstration of transmutation. He then asked if they had continued on their paths as healers. Each one said yes. At last he asked if they trusted him as a responsible teacher. Yes, they replied. As it became clear that the forgiveness he needed was his own, and not theirs, we encouraged him to forgive himself in the presence of the group. Two weeks later, he told us he was more relaxed in his spiritual practices and no longer afraid of vanishing.

CALLING FORTH THE KARMIC BOARD

This technique is extremely helpful when working with a client who carries guilt or shame. The karmic board is a universal council composed of beings who are responsible for evaluating our soul growth and helping us resolve karma's cause-and-effect cycle. From a karmic perspective, human actions are evaluated on the basis of their effect on others; someone who has hurt another person must balance the resulting karma with right action. (*Note:* From a soul empowerment perspective, which embraces a more universal law, all experiences are for soul learning. By clinging to guilt, shame, and judgment of the experience, the individual holds back her soul growth.)

As a healer, you can call forth the karmic board and plead for your client much the same as an attorney would petition a judge and jury on behalf of a client he is representing. You can ask the karmic board to pardon your client and rewrite the records.

You can also ask the karmic board to intervene on behalf of a client whose soul is in jeopardy. Good candidates for this procedure are people who have judged themselves harshly and those under unwarranted psychic attack by an individual or a group.

Charles, an automobile salesman in his mid-forties, had trouble feeling and expressing his emotions. We discovered that in other lifetimes he was a valiant warrior who had killed scores of enemies in battle. Charles, it seemed, was unable to surrender his hyper-vigilance enough to connect with his innermost feelings. Michael, also a former warrior, called forth the karmic board on Charles's behalf. Addressing the council, he stated that he honored and respected Charles as a fellow warrior and a sensitive man. He went on to say that this man had suffered enough and had served his penance. He then requested that his deeds be stricken from the record and that he be given a chance to be a warrior of the heart. Hearing these words, Charles broke down crying.

END-OF-LIFE REVIEW

This review helps to foster multidimensional perspectives on a relationship. Begin by having your client close his eyes and imagine that he has died and is now sitting on a cloud with his guides, relaxing and reviewing his life. Invite him to answer aloud the following questions: "Did you have a soul agreement with _____ in this lifetime?" "What was the precise nature of this agreement?" "Is there anything you wish you had said or done?" "Did you achieve your soul purpose in meeting with _____ in this lifetime?"

Sheila and her young adult daughter, Emily, scheduled an appointment to gain clarity about their constant power struggles. They locked horns during most of the session. At last we asked them the questions listed above. After giving voice to their mutual soul agreements, they cried in each other's arms. Aware that they had agreed to honor each other's individuality, they ended the session with a truce.

INITIATING A REVIEW OF YOUR SPIRIT GUIDES

Here is a technique to use on *yourself*. Guides and teachers come from many dimensions. Some have experienced embodiment on the earth plane, whereas others have not and may not be equipped to furnish the guidance you need. So be sure your guides have expertise in the areas in which you seek assistance. Upon receiving information that does not feel accurate, be aware of your option—and your responsibility—to call in other spirit guides.

If you were about to hire a team of consultants, you would first look into their backgrounds, their experiences, and the fees they charge. So it is with spirit guides. You have a responsibility to your soul to know who is guiding you and what their qualifications are. Ensure that *only* those guides aligned with your soul essence and divine love are allowed to assist you and that all others be blessed and be gone.

Please remember that highly evolved guides abide by the divine law of noninterference. As such, they will not intervene in your evolution unless you request their assistance. As a rule of thumb, we recommend periodically thanking your guides for their assistance and asking God to bless them; requesting that those you have outgrown be lovingly ushered to their next homes; and asking God to send you guides that can truly assist you with your current lessons.

SEXUAL ABUSE CLEARING

People who were sexually abused carry an energetic imprint of the abuse for many lifetimes. The affected energy is most often found around the mouth, throat, breasts, hands, vagina, rectum, and penis.

Energetic imprints can be easily removed through a combination of focused intention, reaching in and pulling out blocked energy, and aura cleansing. If you are working alone, invite the presence of a witness—preferably someone of the same sex as your client. Ask the witness to observe you at all times and to reassure your client of her safety. Explain beforehand that you will not be physically touching your client, but that because you will be working with the trapped energy, she may feel as though she is being touched. Always respect your client's body and feelings.

This work is best performed with the client lying face-up on the floor. To clear the mouth, have your client open her mouth as wide as possible and stick out her tongue. Using the reaching in and pulling out technique, extend your fingers toward her mouth and imagine the energy of your etheric hand reaching into her mouth, throat, and stomach, and gathering and pulling out all the sperm and sexual energy that may have been swallowed and stored in these areas. Repeat the procedure at least three times, then ask your client if she feels clear. If she does not, ask her what she needs to say or do to clear the energy. Allow for whatever is needed, then repeat the technique.

In extreme cases, apply moderate pressure to the stomach, pushing upward toward the throat and mouth, and being careful to bypass the breasts. Long-suppressed emotions may be released in a hysterical outburst. Or your client may gag, cough, feel sick, or even throw up. Keep tissues and a wastebasket handy!

To clear the breasts, use the aura cleansing technique, keeping your hands at least 6 inches (15 cm) from your client's body as you move them from her shoulders to her waist. While cleansing the entire area, imagine that attached to your hands are large brushes wiping clear all imprints of inappropriate touching. Repeat this motion at least three times before asking your client if she feels clear.

To clear the hands, use the same technique described above for the breasts, moving your hands from your client's wrists to her fingertips. Clear one hand at a time.

To clear the vagina and rectum, use the reaching in and pulling out technique, placing your hand at least 6 inches (15 cm) from these organs and follow the procedure for clearing the mouth. Sense the energy from your etheric hand reaching into these areas and gathering sperm or other sexual residue. As you remove your etheric hand, imagine it pulling the blocked energy out of your client's body.

To clear the penis, use the aura cleansing technique, keeping your hands at least 6 inches (15 cm) from the stomach and moving down toward the thighs.

Because almost all your clients will have spent some lifetimes experiencing male consciousness and others experiencing female consciousness, be sure to clear *all* areas of possible sexual abuse. Following the clearing, cleanse the auric field: Keeping your hands 3 to 6 inches (7.5 to 15 cm) from your client's body and starting about 12 inches (30 cm) above her head, move your hands all the way to her feet, allowing the "brushes" to cleanse her entire energy field. Complete the healing session by sealing the aura.

Sexual abuse clearing is a major energetic and psychological experience. The time required for integration may therefore be longer than usual. Please be sensitive to however much time your client needs.

SEVERING CORDS AFTER A MISCARRIAGE, ABORTION, OR EARLY DEATH OF A CHILD

A child's health and life span are dependent on the needs of the child's soul, not on the desires or expectations of the parents. Children enter the earth plane to learn, work through karma, and grow spiritually. Sometimes they come to teach their parents a lesson.

Before entering the earth plane, they consciously choose their life lessons. The more challenging these lessons are, the more the child is likely to grow. Parents, themselves, have agreed to these experiences. (*Note:* Miscarriage, abortion, and early death are all cocreative decisions made between parents and children. In each instance the soul knows what the individual is capable of learning and never creates a setup for disaster.)

Many times when a pregnancy is not carried to term or a child dies at a young age, the child's soul is held back by the parents or other loved ones. This is especially true of a mother who holds on to the spirit of her child out of guilt, shame, or unwillingness to let go. In such instances both the mother's and the baby's evolution are held back, bound by a cord that must be severed for them to continue to grow. (For a firsthand account of this experience, read Rosalie's book, *Healing Grief: A Mother's Story.*)

Natalie, a forty-eight-year-old photographer, came for help after losing five children before their sixth birthdays. Two of the deaths were due to miscarriage; the other three, to early death. Natalie's self-esteem was extremely low, and she was sure she had been cursed by God.

As we established contact with each of her children, the room filled with unconditional love. Each spirit thanked her for allowing it to come and complete what it needed to do. One by one, they acknowledged her pain and reassured her that she was a gift, not a curse. As each one was blessed and released, we had Natalie take a deep breath and exhale the child's energy. When she exhaled, we clapped to cut the cords to the child. By the end of the session, Natalie had released her guilt and acquired an appreciation of the role she had agreed upon playing with the five spirits.

Spiritual Abortion

This technique, like the previous one, honors both the mother and the spirit of the child. Combining dialoguing, forgiving, cutting psychic cords, and other procedures, it helps release the spirit of an unborn child without provoking the maternal guilt, shame, or trauma associated with physical abortion.

Begin by asking the mother if she is willing to communicate with her unborn child's spirit. If she is, ask her to close her eyes, relax, and call forth the spirit of her child. If it does not come in easily, ask the mother to take slow, deep breaths and relax even more fully. When she is entirely at ease, have her again call forth her child's spirit. As soon as she makes contact, remind her that spirit, regardless of its bearer's age, has intelligence and an ability to communicate. Have the mother then ask her child's spirit if it would be willing to communicate with both of you.

Once the interaction begins, encourage the mother to apologize to the spirit for opening the doorway to the womb and explain that the pregnancy cannot be carried to term. (The reason for terminating the pregnancy need not be conveyed unless it will help your client release guilt or shame.) Have her gently reassure the spirit that she does not wish it harm. She may also want to ask the spirit why it originally came—what it needed to learn and to teach. All the while, persist in asking the mother how she is feeling and what the spirit is saying. Her responses are apt to bring suppressed emotions to the surface.

Usually, the spirit of a child whose amniotic life is to be terminated will inform the mother that it only needed to be in the womb a short time. Such unborn spirits consist of those sensing the earth's vibration for the first time, those completing a short segment of an unfinished past lifetime, and those attempting to assist in their parents' education. In each instance the message they convey tends to elicit an emotional release in the mother. The spirit will then thank the mother for allowing it to fulfill its purpose.

At this point in the session, call forth the angels from the schools of wisdom. Inform the child's spirit that these angels will guide it to the schools of wisdom, where it will receive additional healing and teachings, or to an appropriate mother-to-be. Invite your client to surround the child with white light and unconditional love. If the spirit is resistant to leaving, remind it that it cannot stay where it is not wanted, and that by departing now it will not be subjected to the trauma of physical abortion. If it is willing to leave, have the mother imagine the child departing with the angels. Then ask her if she and the spirit have disengaged completely.

If your client appears immersed in guilt or shame, gently remind her that her suffering is holding back her evolution as well as the child's. Assist her in forgiving herself and letting go of the pain. If the spirit's release is further delayed or incomplete, check for soul agreements or cords that may be binding the two together. To break a resistant cord, use the clapping technique.

In our experience with spiritual abortions performed in the first trimester of pregnancy, most mothers spontaneously miscarry within days of the session. Those who go on for a physical abortion emerge from the procedure guilt-free and untraumatized.

Thirteen

UNCOVERING AND RELEASING ENTITIES

• •

"Real suffering burns clean; neurotic suffering
burns more and more soot."

—Marion Woodman

AN ENTITY—a consciousness without a body—is either a
deceased person who continues to cling to his limited human
self, including his earthly attachments, or an energy from
the astral plane. Entities, like human beings, exhibit a broad range
of consciousness. Some carry a remembrance of light and believe
they are truly serving their embodied host or hostess, while others
have no consciousness of the light or of a lifetime on the earth, and
are driven largely by narcissistic needs. All entities, regardless of
their experiences and motivation, create disturbances when they
attach themselves to a person's energy field. Only when they are
expelled can the individual heal and they, themselves, evolve.

UNINVITED GUESTS

The majority of entities are people who have failed to move into the
light after death. For some, the death was so sudden they did not
realize they were disembodied. Others, unprepared for an afterlife,
became disoriented. Still others, ashamed of actions performed in
their previous incarnation, felt unworthy of moving on, or fearful

of being criticized on the other side. Many were held back by emotional bonds, promises, or unresolved power and control issues. While working with a client whose energy field has been penetrated by entities, remember that the entity as well as the client is in pain and in need of unconditional love and compassion.

Entities with no remembrance of the light require more firmness. They are apt to be motivated by a persistent desire to pursue their earth-based addictions or their need for power or revenge. Lacking a physical body, and therefore unable to indulge their desires, they attach themselves to people who can gratify them. Once affixed, these entities amplify the person's cravings.

The potential origins of a client's entities include the following:

1 dead relatives and friends, particularly those who loved him, tried to dominate him, or believed they knew what was best for him—and still do;

2 deceased people who were angry with him or hurt by him;

3 deceased people who had similar issues, emotions, or addictions;

4 the miscarriage, abortion, or early death of a child whose soul has been held back by parental or sibling guilt, shame, or judgment;

5 soul agreements made to protect, watch over, or guide him, which may be either outdated or ill-suited to his current lifetime.

Entities seek energy and space. They are attracted to a human energy field in a number of ways. For one, they gain entry when a person experimenting with psychic energy has neglected to surround himself with intense white light or fails to work only with energies aligned with his essence and divine love. For another, they are drawn in by attenuated anger, jealousy, or denial; refusing to take responsibility for oneself; or failing to remain in one's body. Other attractions include depression, accidents, operations, trauma, abuse, prolonged illness, addictions, and the death of a family member or friend.

Some entities are merely looking for a place to live. They will seek out an unsuspecting person, especially one who is sympathetic and energetically open. Having found the right candidate, they will fasten themselves anywhere between the outermost layer of the auric field to a point deep within the person's body. In the first instance, the attachment will be weak and will drain energy from the aura. In the second, the entity will time-share the body, pushing out portions of the person's consciousness.

Entities are also attracted to the light radiated by human beings, like a moth is drawn to a flame. Many of these unenlightened forms of consciousness are searching for help, because they are lost in time and space. Some, having previously attached themselves to human beings, were cleared by healers who sent them "to the light," never realizing that human beings *are* the light. (*Note:* If you send entities to the light, someone else may inherit them. Instead, send them back to the source so they can evolve, or send them off with the angels to the schools of wisdom so they can be further educated and healed.)

Entities are all around us. If you remain in your physical body, keep your energy field strong, and stay aligned with your essence, your chances of attracting an entity are minimized. If, however, you dilute the strength of your energy field through negative thinking, drug or alcohol abuse, or other addictions, you will most likely open a portal for their entry. If you have suffered from an illness or emotional setback and your energy level is compromised, you may not be strong enough to protect yourself against an attachment. Please remember that you are a multidimensional being and as such have dominion over your body, your energy field, and your experiences!

While meeting with a client always be on the lookout for entity attachments. Signs include sudden uncharacteristic behaviors, such as ungrounded fears, anxieties, depression, anger, or rage; low energy levels; unexplainable allergies or illnesses; personality changes or mood swings; inability to break free of addictions; frozen emotions; confusion; poor memory; and inability to concentrate.

In almost all cases of chronic fatigue syndrome (ME), major illness, or persistent challenge that we have treated, the clients had one or more entities draining their energy. The majority of these attachments had taken place soon after a trauma—usually the death of a loved one—or a personal setback that was either physical, such as an illness, injury, or operation; emotional, such as the breakup of a relationship; or financial, such as losing a business or a home. A good question to ask a chronically ill client is, "Did someone you love die, or did you experience a misfortune, within the three years prior to the onset of your illness?" If the answer is yes, consider the possibility of an entity attachment.

BREAKING THE ENERGY CONNECTION

Entities that affix themselves to living beings establish an energetic connection with them. Some live parasitically, draining the person of all vitality. Others live codependently, stimulating and being stimulated by negative thinking or addictive behaviors. Still others initially provide support and friendship, and have genuine feelings of love for their host or hostess. All entities, regardless of their intentions, drain energy from their host and ultimately hold back their host's spiritual growth.

Confirming the Presence of an Entity

If you suspect that a client with whom you are working has an entity attachment, have your client relax, breathe unconditional love into her heart, and invite the heightened presence of her spirit guides. Then ask her, "Is there an energy or entity in your energy field or in your body that is not *you*?" If she says yes, you can safely assume she is right. If she says no, pay close attention to her body language and possible energy shifts; be on the lookout for body jerks, tightening of the face muscles, or eyes moving into construct mode. You can also use Kinesiology to check for the presence of an entity.

If you have asked your client about the presence of an entity in her energy field and she appears confused, or cannot give you a yes-or-no answer, ask her to close her eyes, relax, take a few deep breaths, fill herself with intense white light, and quiet her mind. When you know she is relaxed and centered, have her go "inside" for the answer. In response to an answer of yes, ask your client's mind to step aside and allow the entity to speak through her.

This technique works well whether or not the person knows anything about entities. About 80 percent of clients will give you accurate information. Those who cannot may relay a signal letting you know their energy field has been penetrated by an entity that insists on remaining undetected. To communicate with a strong and controlling entity of this sort, you will need to be more commanding. Tell your client, "I want to talk to that energy with you that is afraid to let you recover your health (be successful, fall in love, bear a child)."

Seldom will a person have only one entity. Once the human energy field is penetrated, it becomes vulnerable to other entities. Therefore, be sure to ask your client how many entities there are in her body and her energy field. Check with your inner guidance to be sure you receive the same number. Muscle testing can also help you validate the accuracy of her reply. If you note a discrepancy between the information she provides and the responses you elicit through intuition and muscle testing, repeat the question. Once you have determined the number of entities present, you will have a better idea of how compromised your client's energy field is and the amount of release work it requires.

Dialoguing with the Entity

Now direct your questions to the entity. If several are present, start with the one most willing to communicate. Whether it is the soul of an unborn child, the soul of a deceased person, or a negative energy, remember that it has the ability—and perhaps even the desire—to dialogue with you. If the entity refuses, offer reassurances that you will in no way hurt it, then ask again if it will communicate with you.

To establish a dialogue with the entity, begin with an "eye lock." Fixing your eyes on your client's, without blinking or turning away, will amplify your focused intention and weaken the entity's hold. Sustain the eye lock throughout your conversation.

The key questions to ask are these:

1 I would like to talk to the entity in (client's name). I know you are there! Are you willing to communicate with me?

2 How long have you been with (client's name)?

3 More than this lifetime? How many lifetimes?

4 How much of this person's body do you occupy?

5 How do you affect the body and energy field of (client's name)?

6 When did you first come to (client's name)?

7 How did you gain access to this energy field?

8 Why did (client's name) let you in? What did you offer (client's name)?

9 Why did you choose (client's name)? What do you want or need from (client's name)?

10 How many other entities are in or around (client's name)? Will they leave with you?

11 What do you need from (client's name) to be complete and leave?

12 Are you willing to leave peacefully?

13 Is there anything you wish to say to (client's name) before you go?

After dialoguing with the entity, unlock your eyes and return your attention to your client. Ask her if she heard the conversation, and if so, how she feels about having this entity with her. Does she want to say something to it, or express any feelings, such as gratitude, anger, grief, or forgiveness?

Invite your client to tell you, in as much detail as possible, the difference she now feels between her consciousness and the energy of the entity. Ask her what the entity has cost her, and help her understand why it was drawn to her. Finally, ask her if she is ready to take full responsibility for her life or if she wants the entity to remain. Have her state her choice clearly—otherwise, when the entity is released, she may pull it back in. (*Note:* Never remove an entity before the client has learned her lesson from it. Also avoid removing an entity without the client's permission. Once permission has been granted, support the client in taking responsibility for the lift-off.)

Most entities approached in this manner will depart without causing trauma. Only when the person has identified with an entity or experienced it as a true friend does an attachment become difficult to sever.

Releasing Weakly Attached Entities

To release entities that are not deeply attached, use the energy clearing sequence described in chapter 11. Alternatively, try assessing the consciousness of the entity with which you were dialoguing and present it with an irresistible offer. If it can remember a specific lifetime, invite the souls of those who loved it to draw near and help with the release. If it is confused, offer clarity; if it is tired, offer rest; if it is bored, offer additional learning. If the entity is in need of healing, offer to engage the services of healing angels from the schools of wisdom.

Do your best to assist the entity in its evolution. Do not, however, commit to anything you cannot guarantee. Do not ensure that it will be born with its own body, for instance. Instead, explain that when it graduates from the schools of wisdom its records will be reviewed and requests for embodiment will then be considered. Reaffirm that it will receive love, support, healing, and fair treatment.

Follow up your offer with a prayer requesting that the dimensional doorways be opened, and invite the angels from the schools of wisdom to come forth. Ask the angels to escort all entities to the schools of wisdom to be honored for all they have learned and taught, yet not judged, condemned, harmed, or punished in any way.

Releasing Strongly Attached Entities

Entities that are less apt to depart, due to either entity or client resistance, require additional measures. When an entity is too scared to leave, for example, we offer it a parchment scroll inscribed in ink, guaranteeing its safe passage to the schools of wisdom. Before presenting it, we roll it up and tie it with a ribbon.

If the entity still refuses to leave, we remind it that divine and karmic law prohibits it from remaining where it is not wanted and so it must depart. To implement this technique, have your client declare: "By divine and karmic law, you cannot stay where you are not wanted. In the name of God I command you to be blessed and be gone from my body and my energy field right now!"

Just prior to the entity's departure, your client may exhibit grief or other emotions. If the entity was a best friend, she may voice her appreciation. All emotions expressed at this time help to disengage the person's emotional ties to the entity.

When a client wants to release an entity but is fearful of letting it go, ask her what she is afraid of, which personality aspect is holding it back, even how she would benefit by allowing the entity to stay. The moment she realizes that she can take care of herself without the entity, it will have nothing to hold on to. You can then release it using one of the two techniques described below.

The Exhalation Technique—One way to appeal to a firmly entrenched entity is to rely on the information gleaned in your dialogue with it. Knowing why it was allowed in, what it needs for completion, and why it is unwilling to leave will help you select an effective course of action.

After dialoguing with the entity, or after it has loosened its hold enough to be expelled, it is time for the release. Start by calling in angels from the schools of wisdom to help with the lift-off. Then have your client breathe in intense white light, unconditional love, her soul affiliations, and her essence, filling herself completely to loosen the hold of the entity. Finally, have her inhale fully and, on the exhalation, forcibly blow out the energy of the entity. The clapping technique can be used to sever any cords you detect. Repeat this procedure three times if needed, always checking with the client, your intuition, and muscle testing to confirm that the release has taken place. When all entities have departed, have your client fill her energy field once again with intense white light, unconditional love, her soul affiliations, and her essence to lessen the risk of an entity return.

If the entity cannot be released, or if it is too strong for you, do not do battle with it, as this may only cause it to strengthen its grip. Simply provide your client with as much information as possible and encourage her to take more responsibility for her body and energy field. Remember that on some level, they have an agreement with each other. In time, as your client gains insight into her relationship with the entity, she will loosen its attachment so it can be released.

The Starburst Technique—Many deeply embedded entities that are strongly resistant to leaving respond immediately to this technique. Begin by having your client lie down, with her eyes closed. Ask that the dimensional doorways be opened, and call in the angels, as described above. Then have your client imagine four giant aircraft searchlights beaming intense white light at her body. Ask her to breathe in and fill herself with as much of this light as possible. Explain that the light is so intense it will force out all energies unaligned with divine love and her essence.

Then have your client imagine a pinpoint of intense white light, brighter than any she has ever seen, midway between her belly button and the center of her back. Repeat three times: "Make this light brighter. Intensify it even more!" State: "This light is so bright that only those energies aligned with divine love and your essence will remain within the range of its intensity. All other energies will be blessed and automatically released."

Ask your client to imagine the pinpoint of intense white light growing as large as a golf ball, then a grapefruit, then a soccer ball. Have her feel this light clearing out all negativity and discordant energies. Invite her to expand the energy ball until it extends up to her shoulders and down to her knees. Then ask her to expand it further so that it reaches from her head to the soles of her feet. Have her feel it cleansing, blessing, and purifying her entire body. Then ask her to imagine this inner "star" bursting beyond the confines of her body by 3 feet (1 meter), 6 feet (2 meters), 12 feet (4 meters), 25 feet (8 meters), 50 feet (16 meters).

Encourage your client to mentally envision herself surrounded by a capsule about 25 feet (8 meters) away from her body. Explain that it is filled with intense white light and a swirling rainbow of healing colors: gold, pink, blue, violet, green, and yellow. Have her imagine sealing the outside of this capsule so thoroughly that it will guard her against negativity and will accelerate her healing. Tell her the capsule will remain with her for as long as she needs it. Conclude by asking her to open her eyes and describe what she has experienced. (For additional techniques to use in releasing strongly attached entities, refer to our video or audio tape on entity release.)

Spiritual Hygiene for Healers

Entity release work is not for the fainthearted. It requires a high energy level, strong powers of protection, and a thorough knowledge of healing. Why? Because in breaking entity attachments, like striking a hornet's nest, you run the risk of exposing yourself to a brutal attack. (For in-depth information on the behavior of entities, read *The Unquiet Dead* by Dr. Edith Fiore.)

Impeccable spiritual hygiene is a must. On a daily basis, check to make sure your energy field is clear. Any time you notice an energy change, immediately clear it by filling yourself with intense white light. The stronger your energy field is, the more emotionally balanced and protected you will be. And the better you are at monitoring your energy minute by minute, the easier it will be to stay balanced.

If in the course of working with clients you happen to pick up an entity, do not be alarmed and do not judge yourself. Attracting entities is part of the human experience and a distinct occupational hazard. Both of us have picked up entities—from sacred sites, battlefields, churchyards, and shopping malls, as well as client sessions. Sometimes an entity will attach itself to a healer to further its evolution. To disengage from an attachment, dialogue with the entity, call in the angels from the schools of wisdom, and send it off with them.

BREAKTHROUGHS ACHIEVED THROUGH ENTITY RELEASE WORK

Paul, an actor in his late thirties, could feel no sensations in his body. Regardless of the approaches we used, we could not elicit a sensory response from him. We stopped, closed our eyes, and asked for guidance. Almost immediately, we realized that he was sharing his body with an entity.

Michael asked Paul if there was another energy or entity in his body or in his energy field that was not him. With a surprised grin, he said seriously, "Yes, there is." Michael then asked him to relax and energetically step aside so he could speak directly to the entity.

Michael asked the entity how long it had been in Paul's body, how it served Paul, and if it would be willing to leave peacefully. It replied that it had been in Paul's body since he was twelve years old and had come in soon after the death of Paul's father, to help the boy stay strong. It said it would be willing to leave if it were assured of Paul's safety.

When asked if he had been aware of the conversation with the entity and if he wanted its energy to remain in his body, Paul replied that he heard everything and wanted the energy to leave. Michael explained that this energy had served Paul well by helping him maintain his strength, but that it protected him by deadening his sensations. He then asked Paul if he was willing to risk being more receptive to his feelings.

Paul was uncertain, so Michael asked if he would like two angels to support him in learning about his emotions. Paul agreed to the idea, explaining that he would feel safe if assisted by angels. Their presence, Michael knew, would also satisfy the entity's need to know that Paul was protected. Michael then summoned two angels skilled in grappling with emotional energies.

Once the angels were in place, it was fairly easy to release the entity. Two additional entities vacated without resistance. Paul's face flushed as they left, and throughout the remainder of the session he was emotionally responsive.

Jim, a married man in his mid-fifties, described himself as a competent business professional victimized by a sexual addiction that was costing him everything he valued in life. He hated himself for having repeatedly deceived his family and was deeply ashamed of his behavior. Although he had completed residential programs for addiction and participated in group aftercare, he continued to have one-night stands. His wife was ready to divorce him, and his relationship with his three teenage children was in jeopardy.

Jim told us that although he was not sure he believed in entities, he was willing to give the release work a chance, because nothing he had tried thus far had affected his behavior for more than two days. We assured him that he did not need to believe in anything; he simply needed to be present and honest.

We began by introducing Jim to a few simple breathing techniques, which set him at ease. We then asked his permission to invite his guides and teachers further into his energy field, and explained that we would be using them as consultants during the session. He sobbed, muttering that he had felt completely alone, cut off from his inner guidance, and damned. The moment he sensed the energy of his guides, he closed his eyes and relaxed once again.

Jim agreed to let his guides amplify his soul frequency so he could feel his essence. As soon as we noticed his face softening, we asked him to describe the soul qualities he was picking up on. Without hesitation, he replied, "Clarity, sensitivity, ambition, and intensity." We asked if he was willing to have these qualities amplified even more and to become so familiar with them he would be able to recognize them amid hundreds of other energies in the Empire State Building. He agreed, his guides set to work, and within minutes he announced that he felt confident in his ability to recognize his soul qualities.

We then asked Jim to place in a nearby chair each of his conscious thoughts, attitudes, and beliefs that was in alignment with his essence. When he completed the task, we told him we wanted to speak to whatever elements remained in his consciousness. Instantly, he bolted to an upright position, opened his eyes, and stared at us. His unblinking eyes and ramrod posture alerted us to the presence of an entity.

> "Hello," Rosalie said, matching his intensity, practicing eye lock, and sustaining the frequency of unconditional love.

No response.

> "How long have you been with Jim?"

"A long time, longer than you have been alive," the entity said sternly. Its words were clipped, and its tone of voice belligerent.

"Longer than this lifetime?" Rosalie continued.

"You tell me, since you're the expert here."

"We wish to cooperate with you, not do battle. Any information you are willing to share will help."

"I'm confused—maybe longer than this lifetime."

"Thank you for communicating with us. We have no desire to hurt or judge you. We are here to assist both you and Jim."

No response.

"Because you have been with Jim for such a long time, I'm wondering how you serve him."

"I give him companionship. He can always count on me for excitement."

"What initially attracted you to him?"

"His need for intensity and adventure. I am his adrenaline rush. Without me, he would lead a humdrum life, like most of his friends."

"What feelings do you have for Jim?"

"I have no feelings for him. He just serves me."

"How does he serve you?"

"He satisfies my cravings for sex, alcohol, and excitement," the entity said, disclosing the codependent nature of this relationship in which each one kept the other stimulated.

"Do you have any memories of your last lifetime on earth?"

"No."

"How much of Jim's energy field do you occupy?"

"It depends. Sometimes as much as ninety-two percent."

"That's a lot. You must feel very powerful at such times."

"I do, but now that I can predict his every move, he's not much of a challenge."

"We appreciate that you are powerful and that you crave challenges. And we'd like to suggest that there are ways to exercise your power other than by occupying someone's body... Besides, your time is up. You can no longer hide out in Jim's energy field! Once he commands you to leave his body, you must exit, as dictated by universal law. The only choice you have is *how* you will leave—in peace or by force."

"He hasn't ordered me to leave. He needs me. He depends on me as much as he depends on women and booze for his sense of excitement. I've hooked him good."

"You're right, and we don't know if he will order you to leave. If he does, however, we are willing to assist you. Do you know how to move to the schools of wisdom?"

"No."

"Would you be willing to accept our help?"

"It depends. I don't think I'd agree to leave peacefully, since I enjoy living on the edge and combating with humans."

"We will assist you no matter how the lift-off occurs, because this work is part of our soul purpose. We would prefer to assist you in a loving manner so your transition will be easier; however, we are also adept at using our swords and will cut you loose if that is your pleasure. It is your choice."

"I think you're trying to trick me."

"Think whatever you wish. We are here to assist you. We are prepared to offer you safe passage to the schools of wisdom, where you can experience great excitement as you learn about the right use of power. We can promise you not only intensity but also challenges as you learn more about your evolution. While considering this offer, would you be willing to step aside so I can talk to Jim about his responses to this conversation?"

"Do I have a choice?"

"No."

Rosalie took a deep breath, broke her eye lock, and invited Jim to take back from the chair the portions of consciousness that were in alignment with his essence. She instructed him to open his eyes when he felt in alignment with his soul energies. Soon afterward, his eyes opened.

"Hi, Jim," Rosalie said.

He blinked from time to time, though his jaw was more relaxed and his voice quieter.

"Whew, I never expected that," he replied, slumped over in his chair. *"I suspected I carried a blackness, but never before have I felt such heaviness, especially around my genitals and solar plexus."*

"The conversation revealed the impact of the entity, did it not?"

He nodded.

"How do you feel about its ability to override your consciousness, decision making, and will?"

"Out of control—angry and sad."

"You have been seriously out of control. At times, according to the entity, you have been only eight percent present in your body."

"That's very scary. No wonder I have often not felt like myself."

"Look, Jim, you have a right to claim total occupancy of your body and to be free in your own energy field. We can assist, but you are the one responsible for sending the entity away."

"I understand, but who am I without it? You see, it brought me structure."

"Right, Jim, and companionship—and fantasies that cost you your soul and your family. You need to decide if *you* are willing to provide structure for yourself. As for excitement and intensity, you may consult with your guides about activities that are in alignment with your soul. You have not been free in your own energy field for a long time, so this is a big decision. We suggest that you breathe into your soul qualities and let your heart decide."

Jim cried nonstop for ten minutes.

"I have been far from my light for so long and have hurt the people I love most," he finally said. *"I need my light back, especially my integrity, my goodness."*

"Are you ready to send the entity away so you can be in your soul's light? What is your decision, Jim?"

He straightened his back and spoke in a steady, compelling tone of voice:

"I demand that you leave at once. You are no longer welcome in my energy field. Find your own life. I command you to go."

Rosalie asked Jim if he had anything more to say to the entity. After several minutes of silence, he sighed and said:

"Nothing more."

She instructed him to remain present as she returned to her eye lock and invited the entity to speak once again.

"You've heard Jim's command. We're wondering what you are feeling."

"Tired, but strong too."

"Do you have any friends with you?"

"No, though others were expected. My job was to wear him down before their arrival."

Still locking eyes with the entity, Rosalie checked to see if others were in hiding. Satisfied that it was telling the truth, she continued.

"We would like to offer you an opportunity to rest and we want to remind you of the excitement available in experiencing the evolution of your soul. But before you exit, we have a question: Do you have any memory of angels?"

"Sort of. I kind of remember seeing one a long, long time ago."

"We would be happy to call in angels to accompany you as you leave Jim's body."

"Thanks. What's next? How do we do this?"

Rosalie asked for the dimensional doors to be opened to the schools of wisdom and for the entity to be granted safe passage. She then looked lovingly at the entity and said:

"Simply let yourself feel love from the angels as well as your own excitement about your future. I will ask Jim to inhale, hold his breath, then exhale strongly, at which point you will be lifted out. We might clap our hands in his energy field to assist you. Please know that we are not going to hurt you."

"I know that."

"One question before you go... Is there anything you wish to say to Jim? Any sadness you'd like to express before leaving his body?"

"Nope. I don't stay where I'm not wanted. So long, chump."

Rosalie asked Jim to inhale fully, hold his breath, and release it forcefully, blowing out the energy of the entity. She then asked him to breathe in and forcibly exhale two more times, all the while tracking his energy to verify that the release was complete. Next, she invited him to open his eyes.

Rosalie encouraged Jim to remain still for several minutes and to fill his body with his essence. When he seemed ready, she asked:

"How do you feel?"

"A little dizzy, but lighter, like a weight has been lifted from my chest and solar plexus."

"Those are the places where the entity had attached itself, as though it had tentacles reaching into your body. It was deeply embedded within you. Jim, in releasing the entity, we have created a vacuum in your energy field. Nature, abhorring a vacuum, will fill it up immediately if you don't fill yourself up with your own soul values. Are you ready for the final integration piece?" Rosalie asked, chuckling at the word *piece*.

"Sure!"

"If you are willing, please repeat after me, 'I, Jim, from the essence of my being, now call back my clarity, my sensitivity, my ambition, my intensity.'" She then paused and asked, "What else do you wish to call back?"

He replied, *"My power, goodness, and creativity."*

After he invited each energy back, we had him breathe them into his body. At the end of the session, Jim told us he felt more relaxed than ever before, and less lonely as well. He made a commitment to do individual counseling and to ask his family to join him in counseling after he had had an opportunity to discover more about himself.

Fourteen

SAMPLE SESSIONS

* * * * * * * * * * * * * * * * *

*"Why must God be a noun? Why not a verb...
the most active and dynamic of all?"*

—Mary Daly

SOUL EVOLUTION, intuition, and healing strategies all come to expression in the healing session. Most often, only one session is needed to help clients overcome illness, reverse dysfunctionality, manifest their soul purpose, and discover founts of inner guidance. In rare instances, a follow-up session may be required to complete the healing.

Each of the following examples opens with a session summary recording the information we were able to gather by tuning into the client's essence. You, too, will find that as you use focused intention to attune to the essence of your clients, the needs of the soul will announce themselves. You need only remain centered in unconditional love and unconditional thinking, honor the multi-dimensional nature of the person with whom you are working, and trust in the communication process. Each session, you will discover, is like a marvelous symphony that has been composed yet never before performed.

Sample Session 1: Hilary

- ◆ **Challenge or Dilemma**: What to do about work and health
- ◆ **Placement on the Soul Continuum**: Practice lifetime
- ◆ **Soul Purpose**: Communication, creative self-expression
- ◆ **Soul Qualities**: Spontaneity, visibility, freedom
- ◆ **Life Lessons**: Being outrageous, combining diverse forms of creativity, such as drama and painting, movement and poetry
- ◆ **Personality Aspects**: Fear of rejection, perfectionism
- ◆ **Past-lifetime Overlays**: Several lifetimes of intellectual prominence in which creativity was unacknowledged
- ◆ **Healing Approaches**: Breaking past-lifetime vows, forgiveness for judging creativity as inferior to intellect, healing the split between creative and intellectual endeavors, calling back soul qualities
- ◆ **Homework**: Resign from current job; enroll in a clowning, acting, or experiential art class

Hilary, a well-paid researcher in her mid-thirties, consulted us because she had been forced by ill health to take a leave of absence from her job. She described herself as intelligent, energetic, and hard working until her mind and body had suddenly stopped functioning.

When we asked about her placement on the soul continuum, we discovered that she was in a practice lifetime and her soul purpose was to gain awareness of many forms of creative expression. During her previous cycle on the continuum, her guides explained, her soul purpose was to develop and refine her intellect. Toward that end, she had explored science, philosophy, and law. Creativity, she concluded, was frivolous because it was unquantifiable.

As soon as we reminded Hilary that her soul qualities included spontaneity and freedom, she whispered that at the age of twelve she dreamed of being an artist. But her family, giving little credence to her preadolescent "knowing," urged her to invest in her mind.

We suggested that her illness had been triggered by a career that was out of alignment with her soul purpose. She was afraid to try anything she did not excel in, she replied. We reminded her that because she had chosen to embark on a new cycle she was not expected to attain mastery this lifetime. She nodded in agreement.

We completed the session by helping her break the vows she had made to her intellect and by following up with forgiveness affirmations. Reclaiming her inner child gave her courage to heal the split caused by honoring the intellect at the expense of her creative potential. To conclude, we encouraged her to call back her original soul qualities of spontaneity, visibility, and freedom.

A week later she resigned from her job and applied for work as an assistant to a graphic artist. She also enrolled in two evening courses at nearby art college.

SAMPLE SESSION 2: MARK

- **Challenge or Dilemma**: How to break a depressive cycle of rigid thinking and emotional collapse
- **Placement on the Soul Continuum**: Somersault lifetime, shifting from head to heart
- **Soul Purpose**: Emotional development, healing of emotions, emotional balance
- **Soul Qualities**: Empathy, flexibility
- **Life Lessons**: Making self-determined choices, identifying feelings
- **Personality Aspects**: Rigid dualistic thinking, overactivity
- **Past-lifetime Overlays**: A sequence of lifetimes in which either the intellect or the emotions were judged
- **Healing Approaches**: Dialoguing with the soul of his grandfather, self-forgiveness for his perceived involvement in an accident, healing the split between rigid thinking and emotional reactivity, clapping to remove psychic cords, calling back soul qualities
- **Homework**: Create a completion ritual; pay attention to boundaries with respect to responsibility, emotional balance, and integrity

Mark, an oral surgeon in his mid-forties, came to see us because he felt dissatisfied with his life. He confessed that he was rigid and demanding of himself as well as others. When friends confronted him about his controlling behavior, he fell apart emotionally, retreated to his apartment, took the phone off the hook, made himself a gin and tonic, and went to bed—a pattern he had maintained since he was sixteen years old.

When we asked what happened at age sixteen, he sat upright in the chair and clenched his jaw. We encouraged him to breathe deeply. Without a trace of emotion, he then told us his favorite grandfather had drowned while they were sailing together. Mark, who was wearing a life preserver, was pulled out of the water by the coast guard, but his grandfather, who was not, went under.

Although nobody seemed to hold Mark responsible for the accident, he had suffered ever since from survivor's guilt. His parents had ordered him to "be strong and take it like a man," which he tried his best to do. Never grieving the loss of his grandfather, he became a voracious reader and graduated in the top one percent of his high school class. The only place he allowed himself to feel sad was at the movies. He liked to see tragic films, but then embarrassed himself by sobbing.

As we worked with Mark, we encouraged him to respond to us in "feeling" words, hoping to build up his emotional vocabulary. We also urged him to talk to his friends about his grandfather. When the session ended, he said he could not remember feeling so relaxed and excited about his life.

Sample Session 3: Sally

◆ **Challenge or Dilemma**: How to choose a career in alignment with essence
◆ **Placement on the Soul Continuum**: Integration lifetime
◆ **Soul Purpose**: Power, manifestation of ideas and visions
◆ **Soul Qualities**: Perseverance, patience, imagination
◆ **Life Lessons**: Following through on decisions, integrating imagination with practicality
◆ **Personality Aspects**: Lack of self-confidence, indecisiveness
◆ **Past-lifetime Overlays**: A previous lifetime spent exploring ideas and places, and never settling down

- **Healing Approaches**: Healing the split between adventure and stability. Breaking old vows, calling back soul qualities
- **Homework**: Create additional ways to learn about faraway places and cultures; exercise self-determination every day

Sally, in her late twenties, scheduled an appointment with us because she wanted to decide upon a career that honored her soul purpose. The group of doctors for whom she worked had recently promoted her to office manager. Her job was fulfilling; she had made many friends there; and she spent her two week-long vacations each year traveling abroad. The day after she received her promotion, however, a relative offered her a job in his new travel agency. Because of her passion for exotic cultures, she became excited about the prospect of a career in the travel industry. She was in a double bind, she said, torn between the security of her present job and the thrill of a new career.

When we inquired about her placement on the soul continuum, we were informed that she was in an integration lifetime punctuated by several past-lifetime overlays of exploration, with little stability in terms of place or career. Her lessons this lifetime were to follow through on decisions and to experience the continuity inherent in work, family, and relationships.

We told Sally that patience and perseverance were among her soul qualities. She confirmed that her coworkers often admired her self-determination. Altogether, we worked with her for about an hour. When we finished, she smiled and announced that she had decided to accept the promotion as long as she would have six weeks off to travel.

SAMPLE SESSION 4: CARL

- **Challenge or Dilemma**: How to communicate effectively to ensure the success of a business
- **Placement on the Soul Continuum**: Recovery lifetime
- **Soul Purpose**: Power, collaborative leadership
- **Soul Qualities**: Empathy, communication
- **Life Lessons**: Trusting the support of others

- **Personality Aspects**: Fear of making a mistake
- **Past-lifetime Overlays**: A previous lifetime in which ideas were stolen
- **Healing Approaches**: Entity release, breaking past-lifetime vows, calling back soul qualities
- **Homework**: Use affirmations, such as "I enjoy sharing my inventions within the safe parameters of my team"; practice spiritual hygiene to increase personal dominion over his energy field

Carl, an entrepreneur in his mid-thirties, consulted us because his business was in danger of failing due to serious communication problems. Employees were not following through on their tasks and were using many of his business strategies to launch their own part-time enterprises. When we checked for his placement on the soul continuum, we were told he was in a recovery lifetime to heal issues from a lifetime in which business associates had betrayed him by stealing his inventions. He sighed deeply and muttered in a monotone, "For years I've been afraid to trust anyone, especially my managers."

We reminded him that his primary life lesson was to engender support for his ideas, and that failing to communicate effectively with his managers would sabotage these efforts. We added that his empathy, if more readily demonstrated, would compensate for his critical attitude.

At this point, Carl stopped making eye contact with us, and negative energy seemed to fill the room. When we asked him if there was an entity in his energy field, the frequencies about us quickened. As it turned out, he had an entity attachment that was causing him to yell at his managers, embarrassing them in front of one another, and to withhold the incentive pay he had promised them in exchange for their creative ideas. We released the entity and helped Carl break the vows he had made never to allow the ingenuity of others to augment his ideas and inventions. He then decided to share leadership and responsibilities with a team composed of three of his most imaginative managers.

SAMPLE SESSION 5: DAMON

- ◆ **Challenge or Dilemma**: What to do with information and experiences that seem crazy
- ◆ **Placement on the Soul Continuum**: Integration lifetime
- ◆ **Soul Purpose**: Communication, bridging the human realm with the devic realm
- ◆ **Soul Qualities**: Joy, harmony, expanded perception
- ◆ **Life Lessons**: Acquiring comfort in being different, discovering courage to voice expanded knowledge
- ◆ **Personality Aspects**: Wanting to belong
- ◆ **Past-lifetime Overlays**: None
- ◆ **Healing Approaches**: Healing the split between rational and multidimensional perceptions, calling back the devas for support
- ◆ **Homework**: Spend more time in nature; write about personal experiences; assemble a network of friends who experience other dimensions of reality

Damon, a soft-spoken landscape artist in his early twenties, was referred to us because his friends were afraid he was losing his mind. Their concern had piqued each time he told them about the trees, flowers, and even rocks that communicated with him while he was painting outdoors. "I paint the way you channel," he told us with a smile. Then he said he was ready to "chuck everything" and throw himself to nature.

When we tuned into Damon's placement on the soul continuum, we discovered that he was in an integration lifetime and that his soul purpose was to bridge the human and devic realms. After receiving more information, we told Damon that joy and expanded perception were two of his soul qualities. He laughed and said that whenever he is joyful and alive with energies from the nature realm, his friends tell him to "get real."

We went on to explain that his life lessons were about accepting his role as a bridge between dimensions, without feeling pressured to be like everyone else. All three of us then proceeded to describe the rejection we had felt from friends while being most aligned with our soul purpose.

We received no past lifetime information on Damon, which gave us hope that healing the split between the rational and multidimensional modes of perceiving would be simple and effective. As we completed the session, Damon recommitted himself to serving as a channel for the devic realm. Remembering a recurring dream he had had about starting a nature camp for young children, he laughed and said he would invite us to the open house.

Sample Session 6: Bruce

- ◆ **Challenge or Dilemma**: How to find happiness in a relationship
- ◆ **Placement on the Soul Continuum**: Completion lifetime
- ◆ **Soul Purpose**: Healing through personal love
- ◆ **Soul Qualities**: Trust, self-forgiveness
- ◆ **Life Lessons**: Surrendering to sensuality and passion, welcoming healing through love
- ◆ **Personality Aspects**: Control, withholding, denying pleasure
- ◆ **Past-lifetime Overlays**: Several lifetimes committed to celibacy and poverty
- ◆ **Healing Approaches**: Healing the split between personal and universal love, calling forth the karmic board, forgiveness for judging human love as less evolved than divine love, releasing old vows, calling back soul qualities
- ◆ **Homework**: Practice viewing intimate relationships as opportunities for healing

Bruce, an emergency-room technician in his mid-forties, conversed easily, impressing us with his lightspiritedness. At the same time, he exuded an intensity about his inability to sustain intimacy and an urgency to "get it right this lifetime."

When we checked Bruce's placement on the soul continuum, we discovered that he was in a completion lifetime and was committed to his own healing. His guides also told us that his soul purpose was to experience this healing through personal love. When we conveyed the information to him, he wiggled in his chair and admitted that relationships kept taking him away from his "real" work as a student of metaphysics. We smiled and reminded him that empowerment was connected to the *physical* realm this lifetime, that passion and sensuality were his pathways.

"You'll probably think I'm nuts, but I trust the universe more than I trust a lover," he replied. We then learned that Bruce had spent a couple of lifetimes as a monk sworn to celibacy and poverty. Personal relationships were forbidden by the order. Love of the divine, it turned out, was a life lesson he had already mastered, and it was now time for him to feel love's healing power within relationship.

After healing the split in his consciousness and helping him to break his old vows, we called forth the karmic board to pardon him for his arrogance in judging human love. Bruce left the session with a plan to call his most recent partner and express his desire to re-establish a relationship with her.

Epilogue

DISEASE DEVELOPS when the soul and its form of expression is out of alignment with the physical body and its form of expression. Disease always begins in the emotional body. From there it moves inward, affecting tissues, muscles, bones, nerves, or major organs. Another way to understand this process is to recognize that any part of us that is cut off from love eventually becomes sick, for it is the circulation of the heart's energy that keeps us healthy.

From a soul empowerment perspective, all physical illness is caused by the impaired circulation of love. To confirm this hypothesis, the next time you are ill, ask yourself, "Am I experiencing and expressing love or am I withholding love?" If the latter is true, try activating your intention to love. Increasing the frequency of this intention will restore order to your spiritual, emotional, mental, and physical energy fields.

Our experience after working with thousands of people is that healing always follows a shift in awareness—most often an expansion in either unconditional loving or unconditional thinking. We have also observed that healing reinstates one's latent sense of divinity. Many people speak of their healing experiences in terms of "grace," the active expression of God's unconditional love.

Ultimately, healing is accepting your own capacity for grace. As such, once you have experienced a healing, be sure to continually transform your life by transmitting the energies of love to every part of your consciousness as well as each soul you meet.

Appendix A:
Commonly Asked Questions

Q *How does the soul empowerment model work?*

A Energy follows need; we follow the energy once it manifests as information. To receive information emerging from our essence, we must let go of preconceived assumptions, beliefs, and ideas. To receive communication from another person's essence, we must do the same. It takes courage to follow inner guidance. Skill and experience help, too!

Q *How do I know if the information I receive is coming from my intuition or my personality?*

A Practice using your intuition and observing the results; feedback is essential in mastering any skill. Keep a notebook of each "knowing" you have, the action you take, and the outcome you observe. Remember, intuition communicates lovingly; personality demands. Ask your guides for a signal indicating that they are the ones conveying the information. Take joy each day in embracing your intuition. Reserve time for this faculty, just as you would for a best friend.

Q *What happens if I do not accomplish my soul purpose?*

A You will return to this plane with the same soul purpose, though more intense experiences. Once you have accomplished your chosen objective, you will evolve to fulfill a new soul purpose. Returning with the same soul purpose is akin to repeating a grade in school because you did not learn the basics. The choice is always yours: You can procrastinate or you can exercise your free will.

Q *Can you heal me?*

A We do not heal anyone; only you and God can heal you. We can assist you by giving you information about your illness from a multidimensional perspective. We can work with you to release the beliefs, vows, and traumas precipitating your distress. However, the magnitude of your healing, like the severity of your illness, depends on your commitment to aligning with your essence.

Q *I am an active substance abuser. Will you see me?*

A No. Alcohol and drug abuse attract negative energies that undermine the soul's expression and sabotage the healing process. Unless you commit to your own healing by refraining from substance abuse, *we* are not willing to commit to it.

Q *Can you help me without causing me more pain?*

A Struggle and pain are signs that you are out of alignment with your soul purpose. The degree of pain you currently experience reflects the amount of energy that is blocked. Actually, you may feel increased pain for a moment or two as this energy is released. After the breakthrough, however, healing will begin and most, if not all, of the pain will disappear. For now, you may wish to examine the benefits you are deriving from staying stuck in pain.

Q *Is it harder to heal major illnesses, such as cancer and chronic fatigue syndrome (ME), than minor ailments, such as pain and tension?*

A In our experience, major illnesses are sometimes cleared more easily than minor ones. The key is not the severity of the illness, but rather the willingness of the person to take responsibility for himself and align with his essence. This is the initiative that leads to healing.

Q *I'm too scared to come. What shall I do?*

A Come anyway! The fear you feel is your personality putting up a struggle to keep you from healing. If you let your personality win, it will continue to control you. If you take a deep breath and commit to your well-being, it will not. Once you make the commitment, your soul as well as your guides and teachers will support you.

Q *What if I find out that I did something evil in a past life?*

A We have all made mistakes! Remember, we are here to learn and to become specialists in love, power, and discernment. Only by forgiving ourselves can we evolve.

Q *Who will I be when I heal?*

A Your true self—free, happy, creative, and joyful.

Q *My family doesn't believe in the existence of a soul. Is it appropriate to tell them about my healing session?*

A You may not be able to. Instead, share your experience with supportive people, or spend time writing about it. Let your changed behavior, rather than your words, show your family the strides you have taken.

Q *How do I know the healing will last?*

A You won't. Only time will tell. Our job is to help you clear your energy field. Yours is to keep it clear.

Q *Why bother with past lifetimes?*

A Actually, we prefer to think of *simultaneous* lifetimes—with the past, present, and future all coexisting, interfacing, and at times interfering. The reason for remembering a past lifetime is to recognize a pattern you may have brought into this lifetime. Issues that remain unaddressed can deepen your personality grooves.

Q *My religion doesn't acknowledge past lifetimes. Can you still help me?*

A A belief in past lives is not a requirement for healing. Truly, we have enough challenges to work through in this lifetime without entertaining those of prior existences. Our purpose in accessing past-life issues is to free individuals so they can fulfill their current soul purpose and soul agreements. Our task is not to prove or disprove multidimensionality, but rather to facilitate alignment with the bylaws of one's being.

Q *My partner may have an entity. Am I safe?*

A Good question! We are constantly exchanging energies with people, especially those with whom we are most intimate. If your partner has an entity, you *are* being affected, and protection is essential. Remember, nothing can enter an energy field that is already full. Your responsibility is to remain centered and in alignment with your essence. Your partner's responsibility is to seek help.

Q *Do you work with children?*

A We are all children and also elders. Souls are ageless. In a more literal sense, we do work with children, and it almost always involves the entire family. The reason is that children, because they are psychically open, carry the unresolved issues for the family.

Q *What is karma and how do I know if I have it?*

A Sorry, there is no test for karma! We think of karma as the measure of a person's connection to or disconnection from her essence. Others describe it as the fulfillment of the law of cause and effect carried over from one lifetime to the next. However you choose to think of this spiritual principle, remember that "kind karma" exists as well as its more illustrious counterpart known as "bad karma." We all have karma, and the way to ensure a minimum of bad karma and an abundance of kind karma is to stay in alignment with the organizing principles of your soul.

Q *Why do you charge money for healing sessions? Aren't your talents a gift from spirit?*

A All skills are a gift from spirit. As professionals, we take responsibility for ourselves by charging rates comparable to those of other health professionals doing similar work.

Q *How many sessions will I need?*

A Several major issues can be cleared in an hour-long session. The deciding factor is you. If you require a substantial amount of time to integrate healing energies, or if you wish to proceed slowly, a second or third session may be recommended. If your integration is more immediate and if you abide by the suggestions for follow-up care, you may never need a second session.

Q *Aren't you exhausted after a session?*

A No—in fact, we are energized. Interacting with a person's essence can be enormously invigorating. Moreover, the release work itself offers a gratifying opportunity to witness people tapping into their authentic forms of self-expression.

Q *How do the medical and psychotherapeutic communities view your work?*

A Every day, more and more health-care professionals are seeking answers through soul empowerment. Many have come to us for personal healing and gone on to refer clients and family members to us. In addition to private sessions, we offer classes, supervision groups, and supportive videos.

Appendix B:
Helpful Meditations

Relaxing Meditation

Taking a few gentle, nourishing breaths, recall the first day of spring. Breathe in the fresh, warm air. Relax and breathe in your favorite springtime scents. Feel the season's promise of fullness.

As you continue to inhale the energies of freshness and promise, direct them to your heart. Using your breath and focused intention, gently invite your heart to open and receive these energies of renewal. Relaxing even more, take a few moments to enjoy your experience of quiet heart... full heart... understanding heart... compassionate heart... passionate heart.

Feel the radiance that comes with an open heart. Now imagine a large mirror in front of you. Looking into your eyes in the mirror, connect even more deeply with your inner radiance. Returning your focus to your open, welcoming heart, ask yourself, "Who or what does this radiance serve?"

As you continue breathing gently and maintaining an open heart, bring your awareness to your mind. Take a few moments to appreciate the many ways in which your mind serves you each day. Using your breath and intention, gift your mind with the freshness and clarity of the first day of spring. Little by little, experience the presence of gentle mind. Feel yourself trusting the gentleness of your mind. When you are ready, ask yourself what your life would be like if you approached it with a gentle mind. Once again, imagine a large mirror in front of you. Look into your eyes and experience your gentleness. Then imagine a wave connecting your radiant heart with your gentle mind. Ask yourself, "Who or what does my gentle mind serve?" When you have received information, send out gratitude for the insight.

Recalling the freshness and promise of spring, focus your breath and attention on your physical body. As you continue to relax, take time to appreciate all the ways in which your body serves you. Recall physical experiences that filled you with joy and pleasure, and send out gratitude. Once again, imagine a large mirror in front of you.

Look into your eyes as they radiate pleasure, and breathe in even more joy. Imagine the wave from your open heart and gentle mind caressing your physical body. When you are ready, ask yourself, "Who or what is this joy-filled body serving?" Respond to the reply by sending out gratitude.

Remaining centered in the living energies of an open heart, gentle mind, and joyful body, radiate your blessings. Caress your creativity. Open even more to the energies of eternity. Then remind yourself that you can access this relaxed state of consciousness any time you desire. Express gratitude for this open, gentle, joyful way of being. Now bring your awareness back to your physical body. Gently wiggle your fingers and toes, stretch your torso, and return ready to walk in gentle freshness.

Healing Meditation

Breathe the universal energies of healing into the center of your thinking. Say silently, "Center of thinking, I gift you with the energies of healing, which are your heritage. Take what you need and do what you will with the surplus."

Continuing to breathe in the universal energies of healing, direct them to your third eye, located just above and halfway between your physical eyes. Say silently, "Center of vision, I gift you with the energies of healing, which are your heritage. Take what you need and do what you will with the surplus."

Now direct the universal energies of healing to the center of your heart. Address your heart silently, saying, "Center of my heart, I gift you with the energies of healing, which are your heritage. Take what you need and do what you will with the surplus."

Take a few moments to scan your physical body for other sites of welcome, and treat them to the universal healing energies. Silently announce to these areas, "I gift you with the energies of healing, which are your heritage. Take what you need and do what you will with the surplus."

Continuing to breathe in these healing energies, expand your awareness and send them to the energy fields that surround and sustain your physical body. When you are finished, silently announce to the energy fields that you are gifting them with the universal energies of healing, which is their heritage, and that they may take what they need and do what they will with the surplus.

Filled to overflowing with the energies of healing, allow yourself to receive the combined energies of creativity and manifestation. You may be surprised to feel these energies following the same energetic circuit as the healing energies—traveling from your thinking center to encircle your heart center, surround your physical body, and then connect with your invisible energy fields.

As you continue to breathe gently, affirm the ease of creation. Breathe in the energy of evolution to support the energies of creativity and manifestation. Appreciate the many ways in which your existence is a blessing, then invite the energies of evolution to add their blessings to the blessing you already are. Reminding yourself that the consciousness of healing is forever present and available to you, gradually return your awareness to your physical body. When you are ready, gently stretch your body in any way that feels good.

Multidimensional Meditation

Experience yourself perfectly poised in the center of a blessing circle. Imagine breathing in "yes" as you receive the blessings of the earth which supports you. Using your breath and intention, send your blessing to the earth for all her creations. Breathing more gently, accept the blessings of the circle that surrounds you. Be aware that there is nothing you must do in order to receive.

Take time to receive the blessings that are extended to you. Then appreciate the many ways in which your presence on the earth adds to her blessings. Breathe in the freshness of the earth's energies.

Imagine that attached to your navel is a cosmic umbilical cord connecting you to all other dimensions of experience and expression. Become intimate with this cord: What is its texture, color, temperature, age? Does it have an odor? Does it make sounds? Ask it for information about the multidimensional experiences to which it has been treating you since your birth.

Using your breath and intention, begin to journey through your cosmic connector to various multidimensional realities. With each breath, become more and more comfortable with the energies that await you. Inviting the frequencies of the devas, elementals, inner earth beings, angels, and space beings to enfold you and add their impressions to each of your cells.

With every breath, announce your birthright to participate in the dance of multidimensional reality. Claim your legacy to multi-dimensional beingness. Delight in the awareness that as you say yes to the blessings, all expands.

Greet each belief that has diminished your acceptance of dimensions within dimensions. Simply breathe and delight in your ability to dissolve those that do not resonate with your identity as a multidimensional being. Enjoy the ease of claiming your heritage as you dissolve additional limiting beliefs.

Aligned with the spaciousness of your being, announce your readiness to embrace and express your expanded beingness ever more each day. With each breath, discover more ways to celebrate the multidimensional creation you already are.

Focusing your intention on your physical body, experience it from this multidimensional perspective. If there is something you would like to communicate to your body, take time to do that now. As you pulsate with the energies of many dimensions, shower your physical body with the blessings from your multidimensional beingness. Enjoy yourself as the energies dance and play, frolicking in their affinity for one another. Then, while you continue to delight in your expanded awareness, take a few moments to affirm that you are forever all the energies you have just experienced. Appreciate that by simply saying "yes," you have remembered the connection that has always been and will forever be within your being.

Group Multidimensional Being Meditation

Repeat aloud: "I (your name) acknowledge that I am a multi-dimensional being made up of my human nature and my essence nature. I focus my intention on connecting with all aspects of my multidimensionality that are in alignment with my soul purpose.

"I surrender to the wisdom of my soul. With trust and intention, I consciously quiet my mind, surround my emotions with harmony, and relax my physical body to prepare for meditation."

Repeat silently: "Breathing universal love to my high heart, delighting in the multidimensional aspects of my being, I acknowledge the gifts I have received as well as the gift I am, by saying out loud, 'I claim _____.'

"I believe that love is forgiving. I therefore take this opportunity to practice loving by forgiving myself and anyone I have not acknowledged with love and compassion. In demonstration of my trust in love, I now forgive _____.

"I celebrate my connections to multidimensional beings by knowing that all is in divine order and divine abundance. In honor of my ability to manifest life, I joyfully commit myself to being a living expression of multidimensional creativity. In honor of this commitment, I announce to all energies that are in alignment with the well-being of our planet, 'I am _____.'"

Look into the eyes of another person and repeat, "In your eyes I see multidimensional creativity, and I thank you for your courage, your wisdom, and your presence on the earth during this time of initiation and enlightenment." Looking into the eyes of a second person, repeat the same words.

Soul Affiliations Meditation

Shape your breath by saying "yes" at the top of it as you inhale and "thank you" at the bottom of it as you exhale. Remind yourself that there is nothing to do but receive and relax. Then invite your physical body to relax by remembering a place that has filled you with a sense of safety and beauty. Breathe in the energies of that place, sending out gratitude as you relax even more.

Invite your mind to relax by remembering a time in which it was clear and at ease. Breathe in the energies of an open, free mind, sending out gratitude as you relax even more.

Invite your emotions to relax by remembering a time of harmony. Breathe in the energies of harmony, sending out gratitude as you relax even more.

Giving yourself permission to be surprised, focus your intention on remembering your connections and agreements with other realms that are in alignment with your soul purpose. When you are ready, send out gratitude in advance for already knowing all there is to know about your soul affiliations.

As you continue to breathe gently, invite the energies of the nature realm to fill your consciousness. Acknowledge their presence by welcoming them with love. When you feel the uniqueness of their vibrations, ask inwardly, "Do I have a soul agreement to bridge my consciousness with yours of the nature realm?" If you receive a "yes" answer, ask about the specific nature of your agreement. Breathing gently, ask if there is anything the devic realm needs from you. If you are willing to make a conscious commitment to this realm, affirm your agreement. Gently thank these energies for visiting and bring your attention back to your breath.

As you continue to breathe gently, invite the energies of the elemental realm (fire, earth, air, and water) to fill your energy field. Acknowledge their presence by welcoming them with love. When you feel the uniqueness of their vibrations, ask inwardly, "Do I have a soul agreement to bridge my human consciousness with yours of the elemental realm?" If you receive a "yes" response, ask about the specific nature of your agreement. Remembering to breathe gently, ask if there is anything the elemental realm needs from you. If you are willing to make a conscious commitment to the elemental realm, affirm your agreement. Gently thank these energies for visiting and bring your attention back to your breath.

As you continue to breathe gently, invite the energies of the inner earth and mineral realms to fill your energy field. Acknowledge their presence by welcoming them with love. When you feel the uniqueness of their vibrations, ask inwardly, "Do I have a soul agreement to bridge my human consciousness with yours of the inner earth and mineral realms?" If you receive a "yes" response, ask for the specific nature of your agreement. Remembering to breathe gently, ask if there is anything the inner earth and mineral realms need from you. If you are willing to make a conscious commitment to the inner earth and mineral realms, affirm your agreement. Gently thank these energies for visiting and bring your attention back to your breath.

As you continue to breathe gently, invite the energies of the angelic realm to fill your energy field. Acknowledge their presence by welcoming them with love. When you feel the unique nature of their vibrations, ask inwardly, "Do I have a soul agreement to bridge my human consciousness with yours of the angelic realms?" If you receive a "yes" response, ask for the specific nature of your agreement. Remembering to breathe gently, ask if there is anything the angelic realm needs from you. If you are willing to make a conscious commitment to the angelic realm, affirm your agreement. Gently thank these energies for visiting and bring your attention back to your breath.

As you continue to breathe gently, invite the energies of the space realm to fill your energy field. Acknowledge their presence by welcoming them with love. When you feel the uniqueness of their vibrations, ask inwardly, "Do I have a soul agreement to bridge my human consciousness with yours of the space realm?" If you receive a "yes" response, ask for the specific nature of your agreement. Remembering to breathe gently, ask if there is anything the space realm needs from you. If you are willing to make a conscious commitment to the space realm, affirm your agreement. Gently thank these energies for visiting and bring your attention back to your breath.

As you continue to breathe gently, invite the energies of the divine realm to fill your energy field. Acknowledge their presence by welcoming them with love. When you feel the unique nature of their vibrations, ask inwardly, "Do I have a soul agreement to bridge my human consciousness with yours of the divine realm?" If you receive a "yes" response, ask for the specific nature of your agreement. Remembering to breathe gently, ask if there is anything the divine realm needs from you. If you are willing to make a conscious commitment to the divine realm, affirm your agreement. Gently thank these energies for visiting and bring your attention back to your breath.

As you continue to breathe gently, invite the energies of any other realms you have made agreements with to fill your energy field, provided that they are in alignment with your essence. Acknowledge their presence by welcoming them with love. Breathing gently, inquire about the unique nature of your agreement. Ask if there is anything these realms need from you. If you are willing to make a conscious commitment to them, affirm your agreement.

Breathing in the presence of all realms whose energies you have welcomed, take a few moments to enjoy your multidimensional beingness. Realize that just as you ground yourself in the earth, so too are you free to link yourself with your unique soul affiliations.

Remembering that you can visit with your affiliations any time you wish, bring your breath back to the fullness of your physical body. Imagine all your cells celebrating!

GLOSSARY

Abundance. Ample resources for doing what one needs to do when one needs to do it.

Addiction. The compulsive need for a substance, person, or activity that diminishes one's essence.

Affirmation. A building block of consciousness responsible for strengthening one's essence. Examples: "Love is guiding my life" and "In joy, harmony, and safety, I enter the unknown."

Astral plane. A realm of existence outside of time, which vibrates at a higher frequency than the physical plane and contains free-floating energies and entities; home of the emotional body.

Aura. The invisible energy field surrounding all matter and easily affected by energies, including those emanating from one's thoughts, feelings, and environment; the place where illness first manifests.

Bleedthrough. Overflow from an unintegrated past lifetime that impedes one's ability to be fully conscious in this lifetime.

Chakra. One of seven major energy centers in the auric field that corresponds to a place in the physical body and is triggered by the recall of past-life trauma; a point of attachment for a psychic cord.

Co-arising. An energetic principle that guarantees emergence of the polar opposite of whatever one is affirming. Example: While affirming love, fear will arise.

Conscious feminine. Energy associated with receptivity, nurturing, acceptance, and surrender, as expressed by a woman or a man; a dynamic portrayed by the left side of the body.

Conscious masculine. Energy associated with the intellect, independence, focus, and action, as expressed by a man or a woman; a dynamic portrayed by the right side of the body.

Conscious mind. An aspect of the rational self that filters, weighs, and analyzes; gatekeeper of the subconscious mind.

Consciousness. A reflection of the state of the soul; a memory lens through which one focuses his attention, guides his intuition, and directs his being.

Cord. *See Psychic cord.*

Cosmic report card. An evaluation of one's performance in terms of soul purpose, soul qualities, life lessons, and placement on the soul continuum; a curriculum review compiled in soul space after a physical embodiment.

Defense. A personality dynamic caused by the failure to have one's expectations met in childhood. Examples: resistance, projection, denial.

Dissociation. Avoiding painful feelings by energetically splitting off from the physical body.

Double bind. A lose-lose situation that prevents alignment with one's soul purpose; a communication pattern suggesting the suppression of painful emotions.

Emotional incest. A situation in which parents or guardians consciously or unconsciously use a child for the fulfillment of their own emotional needs; a dysfunctional family pattern that, while unhealed, causes an energy blockage.

Energy blockage. Energy trapped in the body as a result of fear or trauma.

Energy frequency. The rate of vibration of a thought, belief, or feeling. Negativity and depression vibrate at a low frequency; healing and joy, at a high frequency.

Entity. A disembodied or astral energy that attaches itself to a living person.

Essence. Core of the soul; that which remains when the personality has been transformed; one's connection to eternity.

Etheric. The energy residing in a field immediately beyond the physical.

Evolution. The journey of the soul as it seeks growth through time and space.

Frequency. *See Energy frequency.*

Guide. A being who offers assistance from the world of spirit; a spiritual mentor who is attracted by one's needs, lessons, and energy frequency.

Harmony. A state in which spirit can manifest in matter.

Healer. A person who serves as a resource for the source.

Inner child. The part of a person that remains alive, spontaneous, creative, and intuitive, regardless of chronological age or psychological history. Reclaiming the wounded child is a stepping stone to forgiveness.

Intention. Focused attention derived through activation of the will. Lack of intention leads to confusion and failure.

Internal dialogue. The kinesthetic communication channel that connects one to inner voices from past authority figures. Engaging in internal dialogue keeps a person out of touch with her authentic feelings and her true self.

Intuition. The silent voice of spirit that connects the human self with the essence self.

Karma. The measure of an individual's connection to or separation from his essence. Also, fulfillment of the law of cause and effect carried over from one lifetime to the next.

Karmic board. A council of beings who review the karmic records of humanity and decide whether or not individuals have learned their life lessons; a body authorized to grant pardons and rewrite the karmic records.

Kinesiology. A technique for tracking information; specifically, the use of muscle testing to determine whether an energy field is strengthened or weakened by a particular object, substance, or relationship.

Learned limitation. An internalized half-truth that prevents alignment with one's soul purpose.

Life lesson. A course of instruction to be learned over the course of a lifetime.

Matching pictures. A situation in which the healer has an unresolved issue similar to that of the client.

Matter. A condensed form of energy.

Mismatching. A problem in understanding caused by the use of different communication styles.

Neuro-Linguistic Programming (NLP). A technique for tracking information; specifically, the use of sensory cues to evaluate how the brain receives, stores, processes, and retrieves information.

Organizing principles of the soul. Soul values that form the foundation of one's being.

Past programming. The "shoulds" instilled by past authority figures and acculturation; focal point of internal dialogue that obstructs access to one's true feelings.

Personality. The totality of an individual's limited beliefs from past programming that foster a sense of alienation; often synonymous with ego.

Personality aspect. A defense, resistance, or projection that keeps an individual out of alignment with her essence. Examples: anger, control, doubt, impatience, jealousy.

Personality groove. An unconscious pattern of behavior rooted in learned limitations. If unchallenged, a personality groove will obstruct one's capacity to choose and to change.

Polarity. The result of a split in consciousness, causing a dualistic perception. Examples: positive/negative, masculine/feminine, abundance/scarcity.

Power. The energetic surge that arises when one is in harmony with his deepest truths; the capacity to manifest one's desires.

Psychic cord. An energetic attachment to people or places. Psychic cords connect to the chakras, disrupting the individual's energy flow.

Resistance. Unwillingness to move forward and align with essence.

Root cause. The originating circumstances of an issue. Resolving the root cause provides the greatest opportunity for healing.

Soul. The "divine spark" within an individual that contains the cosmic blueprint for her earthly evolution.

Soul affiliation. An allegiance to a being of another dimension. Examples: devas, elementals, inner earth beings, angels, space beings.

Soul agreement. A contract made prior to physical incarnation to further the growth of all participants. A soul agreement may be formed independently or between two or more parties.

Soul continuum. The evolutionary path marking a soul's growth and development.

Soul empowerment. A method of healing that aligns an individual with his essence.

Soul family. A group that shares the same energy frequency and has agreed to work together.

Soul purpose. An inner directive that activates the experiences and expressions needed for the continued growth of the soul. Examples: communication, emotional development, healing, love.

Soul quality. Individualized aspects of spirit that promote healing. Examples: creativity, flexibility, forgiveness, gentleness, self-love.

Soul quality retrieval. A technique used to call back aspects of the soul that one has judged, condemned, or sent away; reintegration promotes wholeness and healing.

Soul space. The dimension that a soul inhabits between lifetimes.

Spirit (Latin, "breath"). The all-knowing, ever-present divine, which gives the breath of life.

Spiritual bypass. A personality strategy used to short-circuit the experience of pain or loss.

Split. Polarity thinking; an either-or dichotomy preserved by consciousness.

Subconscious mind. The nonjudgmental aspect of consciousness that retains a complete record of one's experiences on the earth plane; information is accessed through suggestion.

Superconscious mind. The portion of consciousness responsible for unlimited intuitive wisdom and direct insight into the true nature of things.

Synchronicity. The coincidental occurrence of events; chance encounters; evidence that one's soul purpose has been activated.

Vow. An agreement made in the present or a past lifetime that continues to exert an influence.

Will. The inner drive to become conscious of oneself as a multi-dimensional creator and creation; the mediator between mind and emotions; an energy-dependent force that gains stamina as it is exercised.

BIBLIOGRAPHY

Atkinson, Robert, *The Gift of Stories,* Westport, Bergin & Garvey, 1996.

Baldwin, Christina, *Life Companion: Journal Writing As a Spiritual Quest,* Bantam Books, 1990.

Bandler, Richard and Grinder, John,*The Structure of Magic,* vol.1, Science and Behavior Books, 1989.

Bradford, Michael, *The Healing Energy of Your Hands*, The Crossing Press, 1995.

Caddy, Eileen, *Waves of Spirit*, Findhorn Press, 1996.

Capacchione, Lucia, *Recovering Your Inner Child,* Simon & Schuster, 1991.

DeRohan, Ceanne, *Right Use of Will,* One World Publications, 1984.

Erbe, Peter, *God I Am: From Magic to Tragic,* Triad Publishers, 1991,

Fiore, Edith, *The Unquiet Dead: A Psychologist Treats Spirit Possessions,* Ballantine Books, 1987.

Foundation for Inner Peace, *A Course in Miracles,* Tiburon,1975.

Hay, Louise, *You Can Heal Your Life*, Hay House, Inc., 1984.

Heart, Rosalie Deer, *Healing Grief: A Mother's Story,* Heart Link Publications, 1996.

Hendricks, Gay and Kathlyn, *At the Speed of Light: A New Approach to Change through Body-Centered Therapy,* Bantam Books, 1993.

Keen, Sam, *Fire in the Belly: On Being a Man,* Bantam Books, 1991.

Monroe, Robert, *Journeys Out of the Body,* Doubleday, 1972.

Moore, Thomas, *Care of the Soul,* Piatkus, 1992.

Myss, Caroline, *Anatomy of the Spirit,* Harmony, 1996.

Roberts, Elizabeth, and Amidon, Elias, *Life Prayers: Affirmations to Celebrate the Human Journey,* HarperCollins, 1996.

Roberts, Jane, *The OverSoul Trilogy*, Amber-Allen Publishing, 1995.

Roth, Gabrielle, *Maps to Ecstasy*, Nataraj, 1993.

Satir, Virginia, *Conjoint Family Therapy,* Science and Behavior Books, 1967.

Speare, Grace, *Everything Talks to Me,* Berkley Books, 1982.

Welwood, John, *Journey of the Heart,* HarperCollins, 1990.

Wickes, Frances, *The Inner World of Choice,* Harper & Row, 1963.

Woodman, Marion, *The Pregnant Virgin: Psychological Transformation,* Inner City Books, 1985.

Young, Lady Meredith, *Language of the Soul*, Still Point, 1987.

Index

About the Authors

Rosalie Deer Heart, a psychotherapist in practice for more than twenty years, specializes in psychospiritual integration and women's adult development. She teaches The Spiritual Foundations of Creativity, Soul Empowerment, and Women's Rites of Passage at the Creative Problem Solving Institute of New York University in Buffalo. In addition she is an interfaith minister and a licensed medium. Her previous books include *Affective Education Guidebook: Classroom Activities in the Realm of Feelings* (coauthored in 1975), *Affective Direction: Planning and Teaching for Thinking and Feeling* (coauthored in 1979), and *Healing Grief: A Mother's Story* (Heart Link Publications, 1996).

Michael Bradford, a former corporate president and management consultant, has been an intuitive healer for over 14 years. His unique multidimensional approach to healing incorporates Eastern and Western philosophies, spiritual guidance, and high-vibrational healing frequencies. Author of the international best-seller *The Healing Energy of Your Hands* (The Crossing Press, 1995), Michael travels internationally, leading workshops on advanced healing techniques, prosperity, spiritual development, and soul empowerment. He is a member of the World Federation of Healing and the International Association of Spiritual Psychiatry and cofounder of the Chiron Kentavros Foundation in Greece.

Together, Rosalie and Michael work with individuals, families, groups, businesses, and organizations that are committed to healing from a soul-empowerment perspective. Their dream is to establish centers in which healers from around the world will share their gifts in the spirit of love and collaboration.

ORDER FORM

QUANTITY	ITEM	AMOUNT
_____	*Soul Empowerment:A Guidebook for Healing Yourself and Others* ($15.95)	_____
_____	*Healing Grief: A Mother's Story* by Rosalie Deer Heart ($14.95)	_____
_____	*The Healing Energy of Your Hands* by Michael Bradford ($12.95)	_____
	New Mexico residents, please add 6.875%	_____
	Shipping and handling ($2.05 per book)	_____
	Total amount enclosed	

Discounts are available on orders of 10 or more items.

Ten supporting *Soul Empowerment* videos are also available.
For details, please request an informational brochure.

Please mail your order, together with your name, address, and check or money order, to:

Heart Link Publications
PO Box 273
San Cristobal, NM 87564
800-716-2953

Rosalie Deer Heart and Michael Bradford
thank you for your interest and support.
Please send them this card, or call them at 800-716-2953

I am most interested in the following areas (please check):

Workshops — 2, 3 and 7 day
- ☐ Soul Empowerment
- ☐ Intuition Enhancement
- ☐ Healing Techniques

Specialized Training Programs — 2, 3 and 7 day
- ☐ For Health Professionals
- ☐ For Healers

Apprenticeship Training Programs
— 6 month, 1 and 2 year
- ☐ In person
- ☐ Correspondence course

Healing sessions
— for individuals, couples, families and groups
- ☐ In person
- ☐ Via phone

Soul readings
— for individuals, couples, families and groups
- ☐ In person
- ☐ Via phone

- ☐ **Spiritual Retreats** — 7 and 14 day
- ☐ **Spiritual Journeys to Sacred Sites** — 14 and 21 day
- ☐ **Consulting** — for businesses, companies and organizations
- ☐ **Sponsoring us**
  — I would like to organize a workshop in our area

Rosalie Deer Heart and Michael Bradford
thank you for your interest and support.
Please send them this card, or call them at 800-716-2953

I am most interested in the following areas (please check):

Workshops — 2, 3 and 7 day
- ☐ Soul Empowerment
- ☐ Intuition Enhancement
- ☐ Healing Techniques

Specialized Training Programs — 2, 3 and 7 day
- ☐ For Health Professionals
- ☐ For Healers

Apprenticeship Training Programs
— 6 month, 1 and 2 year
- ☐ In person
- ☐ Correspondence course

Healing sessions
— for individuals, couples, families and groups
- ☐ In person
- ☐ Via phone

Soul readings
— for individuals, couples, families and groups
- ☐ In person
- ☐ Via phone

- ☐ **Spiritual Retreats** — 7 and 14 day
- ☐ **Spiritual Journeys to Sacred Sites** — 14 and 21 day
- ☐ **Consulting** — for businesses, companies and organizations
- ☐ **Sponsoring us**
  — I would like to organize a workshop in our area

affix
stamp
here

Please
write here
your name
and address

(please
PRINT)

HEART LINK PUBLICATIONS
PO Box 273
San Cristobal
NM 87564
USA